fly girls

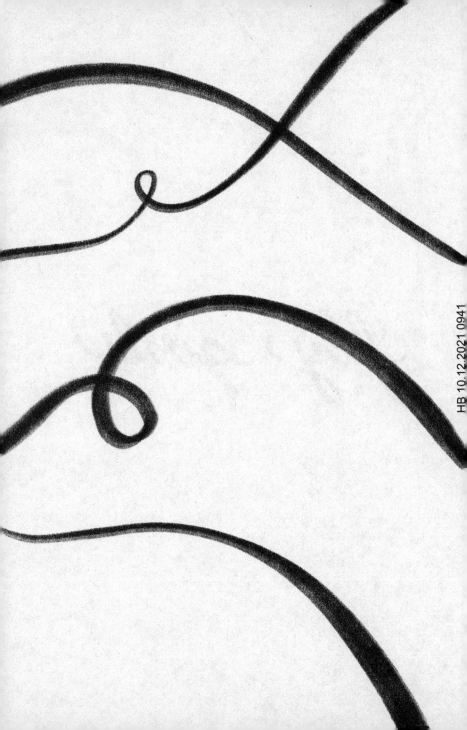

YOUNG READERS' EDITION

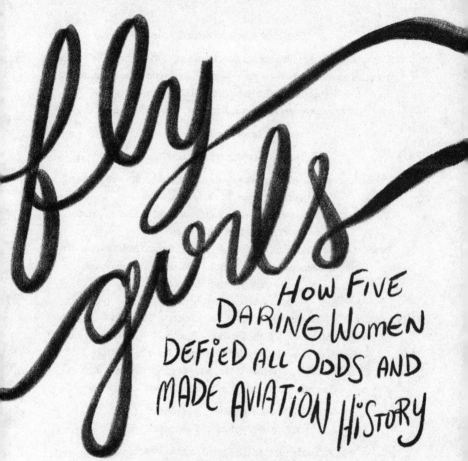

fly girls

How Five Daring Women Defied All Odds and Made Aviation History

KEITH O'BRIEN

Houghton Mifflin Harcourt

Boston   New York

hmhbooks.com

The text was set in FreightText Pro.

The Library of Congress has cataloged the hardcover edition as follows:
Names: O'Brien, Keith, 1973– author.
Title: Fly girls : how five daring women defied all odds and made aviation
history / by Keith O'Brien.
Description: Young readers' edition. | Boston : Houghton Mifflin Harcourt,
[2018] | Audience: 010 & up | Includes bibliographical references.
Identifiers: lccn 2018051352
isbn 9781328639899 (e-book)
Subjects: LCSH: Women air pilots — United States — Biography — Juvenile
literature. | Air shows — United States — History — Juvenile literature.
Women in aeronautics — United States — Juvenile literature.
Classification: lcc tl539 .027 2018c | ddc 629.13092/520973 — dc23
LC record available at https://lccn.loc.gov/2018051352

ISBN: 978-1-328-61842-9 hardcover
ISBN: 978-0-358-24217-8 paperback

Manufactured in the United States of America
2 2021
4500839781

For Mom, Dad,
and that great solo flier,
Grandma

Contents

Introduction   1

PART I

1: The Miracle of Wichita   7

2: Devotedly, Ruth   13

3: An Extremely Interesting Girl   17

4: The Fortune of the Air   23

5: The Fairest of the Brave and the Bravest of the Fair   33

6: The Lion's Cage   42

7: Flying Salesgirls   52

8: The Right Sort of Girl   59

9: Where Is Miss Earhart Now?   69

PART II

10: City of Destiny   75

11: If This Is to Be a Derby   80

12: There Is Only One Cleveland   88

13: Beware of Sabotage   91

14: No Time to Stop   98

15: Good Eggs   108

16: Mr. Putnam   114

17: Law of Fate   117

18: No In-Between   124

19: The Man in the Mansion   128

20: Give a Girl Credit   134
21: Grudge Flight   139

PART III

22: *Spetakkel*   147
23: Anything You Want   151
24: Say Hello to the Crowd   154
25: Her Life for the Show   158
26: All Things Being Equal   161
27: Men Pilots Only   166
28: That's What I Think of Wives Flying   171
29: An Excellent Type of Woman   178
30: They'll Be in Our Hair   183
31: On the Sidelines   189
32: The Chance of a Lifetime   193
33: We Are Going to Fly   198
34: Splinters and a Grease Spot   202
35: Goodbye, Darling   205
36: Sky Ghosts   209
37: A Woman Couldn't Win   212

PART IV

38: Disappointments, Dedication, and Courage   219

Glossary   229
Source Notes   233
Index   295

fly girls

Introduction

Today, traveling by air is one of the safest ways to get from one place to another. Put simply: airplanes rarely crash. But in 1926, when air travel was new, it was different. Planes crashed for all sorts of reasons. Propeller blades snapped and broke. Wings failed, breaking off completely. And all too often, engines just stopped in midflight. "In such a crisis, there is no time to think," said one early aviator. "You either automatically do the right thing or you die."

In clear skies, pilots often made the wrong choice. In bad weather, they had even fewer options. Rain, snow, and fog made flying almost impossible. In open-cockpit planes, raindrops felt to pilots like marbles hurled at their faces at a hundred miles an hour. Goggles fogged up, paper maps blew away in the wind, and aviators got lost. A pilot, in moments like these, was told to find railroad tracks on the ground and follow them. By doing so, a lost flier could find the nearest town.

But flying just fifty feet off the tracks was dangerous too. In one such case, a pilot slammed his plane into a mountain when the railroad entered a tunnel. Worst of all, pilots could do everything right and still lose, for reasons out of their control. In the 1920s, plane builders often used wood to construct their machines, then stretched linen over the wings, like pillowcases. These lightweight materials helped make flying possible. But the wood could rot and the fabric could tear, dooming even the best fliers. As one expert pointed out, "Many pilots have been killed in wood **fuselage** ships."

These deaths worried the **aviation** industry. Planes may have been flying for two decades, but the industry itself was just getting started, really. Most people had never sat in an airplane. And if they thought planes were dangerous, who would fly in them? Who would take the chance? So in the 1920s, the industry started holding events to stir up excitement: airplane races. Small at first, these events quickly grew until pilots were racing against one another in what became known as the National Air Races. Soon, Americans weren't just reading about pilots darting across the ocean; they were watching them race over their own rooftops or across the country in one of the most famous events of all: the Bendix Trophy race. "It has become," one pilot said of the Bendix, "like the World Series."

These races were often fatal for pilots. To win, they had to fly fast and low—sometimes making hard turns around small towers called **pylons.** It was a recipe for disaster and, many men believed, no place for a woman. In the late 1920s, newspapers published articles questioning whether a woman should be allowed to fly anywhere, much less in these races. That such questions could be posed—and taken seriously—might strike us today as ridiculous.

2

But they were all too typical of the time. American women had earned the right to vote only a few years earlier, and laws still forbade them to serve on juries, drive taxicabs, file lawsuits, or work night shifts. It is not surprising, then, that female pilots flew through a storm of insults. They weren't real aviators, as far as the men were concerned. They were ladybirds, flying flappers, and sweethearts of the air. They were just "girl fliers"—the most common term for female pilots at the time.

But in 1926, a new generation of female pilots was emerging, and they refused to be excluded. Instead, they united to fight the men in a singular moment in American history, when air races attracted bigger crowds than opening day at Yankee Stadium and an entire Sunday of NFL games combined. These were no "sweethearts," no "ladybirds." If these women aviators had to have a name, they were fly girls—a term used to describe female pilots and, more broadly, any young women who refused to be told what to do, whom to marry, or where to work, appearing bold as a result.

It's a story that plays out over one tumultuous decade, when so much about America was changing. At the beginning, in 1927, even independent women interested in aviation were considered cargo to be flown by male pilots from point to point. At the end, in 1937, women would compete head-to-head against men in that great cross-country race for the Bendix Trophy. A woman, many believed, could never beat a man in such a race. But in 1936, one woman did, in a stunning upset that finally proved women not only belonged in the air—they could rule.

Among them were wives and mothers, teachers and bankers, daredevils and starlets. And five women in particular: Ruth Elder, a charming wife from Alabama who paid the price for going first; Amelia Earhart, a social worker living with her mother on the outskirts of Boston and looking for a way out; Ruth Nichols, a daughter of Wall Street wealth in New York, who wanted to make a name of her own; Louise McPhetridge Thaden, a dreamer from rural Arkansas who wanted it all—a job, a family, fame—but would have to make a difficult choice; and Florence Klingensmith, a young pilot from the northern plains whose gamble in the sky would change everything for the other women on the ground.

In the decades to follow, only one of these five women— Amelia Earhart—would be remembered. But for a few years, before each of the women went missing in her own way, these female pilots captivated a nation, hoping to beat one another and longing to beat the men. At times, a hundred thousand people swarmed dusty airfields to watch them compete, darting through the sky in their colorful planes—robin's-egg blue and pale orchid; scarlet red and gleaming white—and racing, an impossible tale playing out in a deadly sky.

It began on the Kansas prairie, with a young woman named Louise McPhetridge dreaming of something big.

She wanted to fly.

PART I

CHAPTER 1
THE MIRACLE OF WICHITA

*T*he coal salesmen on the Arkansas River took note of Louise McPhetridge from the moment she appeared in the window by the door. It was hard not to notice her. McPhetridge was young and slender, with a tangle of brown hair and surprising height for a woman at the time. At five foot eight, McPhetridge was usually the tallest woman in the room and sometimes taller than the men she passed on the streets of Wichita, Kansas.

But it wasn't just how she looked that made her remarkable; it was the way she talked. McPhetridge had attended college, and she spoke with perfect grammar. Perhaps more notable, she had a warm Southern accent, a hint that she wasn't from around Wichita. She was born in Arkansas and different from most women in at least one other way: McPhetridge was boyish. That's how her mother put it. Her daughter, she told others, "was a follower of boyish pursuits."

Louise's parents, Roy and Edna, could doll their daughter up in white dresses as much as they wanted when she was a child. Louise would always find a way to change into overalls and get dirty. She rounded up stray dogs. She worked on her father's car engine, and sometimes she joined him on his long car trips selling healing ointments, a job that had finally landed the McPhetridges in Wichita in the summer of 1925. At nineteen years old, Louise found herself living near the coal company close to the Arkansas River.

It was a hard time to be a woman looking for work, with men doing almost all the hiring. "Write, stating age, height, weight and where last employed," employers told women looking for a job. They often wanted the most attractive employee, not the most skilled. But the man who owned the coal company had different standards. Jack Turner was an immigrant from England, who had come to America with just seven dollars in his pocket and then turned it into a small fortune. He argued as early as 1922 that workers should be paid what they were worth, no matter their gender. And he predicted a future where men and women would be paid equally, based on skill. But he was known, most of all, for coal. "Everything in Coal," his advertisements said. "Coal Is Scarce. Fill Your Coal Bin Now."

He hired Louise McPhetridge not long after she arrived in town. And for a while, McPhetridge stayed focused on her job, selling coal. But by the following summer, her mind was wandering, following Turner out the door, down the street, and into a brick building just half a block away. The sign outside was impossible to miss. TRAVEL AIR, it said. AERIAL TRANSPORTATION TO ALL POINTS. It was a small place, but to Louise, the name, Travel Air, was almost magical, and the man working inside was the most unusual sort.

He was a pilot. And his name was Walter Beech.

—

Beech was thirty-five that summer and a long way from his native Tennessee. But he felt at home in Kansas. "I want to stay in Wichita," he told people, "if Wichita wants me to stay."

The reason was professional. In town, there were two airplane factories, and Beech was the kind of person they needed to hire. He had learned to fly and repair airplanes with the U.S. Army in Texas. And thanks to this experience, Beech had become the general manager at the company Travel Air. The small outfit was just getting started building airplanes in Wichita, and Beech's job was to sell them. He was to sell them by winning races, especially the 1926 Ford Reliability Tour, a twenty-six-hundred-mile race across the Midwest. The race would begin and end in Detroit, with stops to refuel in thirteen cities along the way. The winner would be famous. All of Wichita would be watching. And the aviation industry hoped it would prove that planes were a reliable mode of transportation.

"Don't save this motor," the engine man told Beech at the starting line in Detroit that August, urging him to fly as fast as possible. "Let's win the race."

Beech pushed the **throttle** of the Travel Air plane as far as it would go. He was first into Kalamazoo, first into Chicago. With the help of a navigator named Brice "Goldy" Goldsborough flying along with him, Beech flew into the fog around St. Paul—and won yet again. Then he prevailed in Des Moines and Lincoln and, finally, most important, Wichita, the midway point in the race. This time, he beat the other fliers by almost seven minutes despite engine trouble.

"It's certainly good to be back home again," Beech told the crowd of five thousand people after stepping out of the **cockpit**. "The old town looks good to me, and wonderfully restful after the strain of hard, fast flying."

A beauty queen, Miss Wichita, presented him with a golden key to the city. And six days later, back in Detroit, in front of another large crowd, race officials gave Beech a trophy and a check for twenty-five hundred dollars—first place. He and the other pilots had covered a total of 61,000 miles, flying on despite eight accidents and one death, when a plane hit a man on the ground. But if the point of the Ford tour was to prove that an airplane was reliable, Travel Air, with Beech at the controls, had succeeded. At the very least, it had proven this: Beech knew what he was doing.

"Let us consider," he said, "that not every hometown boy is a fool. Let us consider listening to their arguments of what they can do. Pick out a miracle that is possible for them to accomplish."

———

Back in Wichita that summer, McPhetridge tried to do her job, selling coal for Jack Turner. But she was distracted by the news about the races and the planes. She just had to see them for herself.

Day after day, she went to the Travel Air **hangar,** where the planes were stored, in the tall grass east of town. She stuck out amid the grease-stained mechanics and pilots working on the planes, but she felt at home among them. She wasn't a pilot flying a plane. But as a girl back in Bentonville, Arkansas, McPhetridge had longed to pull off miracles of her own.

McPhetridge once jumped from the second story of a barn just to see what it felt like. She drove her father's car long before she was old enough to have a driver's license, and she sometimes did things just because others said they couldn't be done. It was the sort of behavior that got her into trouble at times.

Now, at the airfield in Wichita, McPhetridge was flirting with trouble again. It was only a matter of time before her boss, Jack Turner, caught her there when she should have been selling coal. McPhetridge thought she was going to get fired. Instead, she got a phone call from Walter Beech.

He and Turner wanted to offer her a different job. They wanted her to work for Travel Air's new West Coast salesman, D. C. Warren.

"Warren has agreed to take you out to San Francisco," Beech told McPhetridge at their meeting. "Your salary won't be high, but he will teach you this aviation business and see that you learn how to fly."

McPhetridge was stunned. Her parents were too. They knew their daughter was different. Her mother had even accepted the fact that Louise would never be a traditional woman, the kind who would be happy tending to a home. But this job offer from Walter Beech was too much, even for them.

"Oh, Louise," her mother said, disapproving. Her father wasn't pleased either. He wanted to call Beech to tell him that Louise could not take the job in California. But Louise talked her father out of making the call.

"It is," she told her parents, "the one thing I want to do."

Not long after, in early April 1927, she said goodbye to her family, to her job selling coal, and to everything else in Wichita and climbed into a Travel Air plane headed West. It was cold in Wichita that morning, almost freezing. Yet the sky over the prairie was blue, giving McPhetridge a clear view of the ground from the passenger seat of the little plane bound for the coast. By nightfall, she had reached San Francisco.

CHAPTER 2
DEVOTEDLY, RUTH

A cross the country from McPhetridge in California, another young woman wanted to make a move of her own. She lived in a house so big it required no street number. The Nichols family gave their address as simply Grace Church Street, Rye, New York. The home was about twenty miles from midtown Manhattan. Visitors couldn't miss it—all three stories of it.

But inside, the house was dark and scary. Dead animals mounted on the wall stared down on everyone. A grandfather clock ticked away, ringing on the hour. In the dining room, children were expected to behave while the family ate off fine china. And any child who broke the rules might be forced to answer to the owners of the house, Erickson and Edith Nichols, and possibly sent to dine with the family's servants. In 1925, there were three of them.

The oldest child, a daughter, had at least one thing going for her: she wouldn't be there for long. Ruth Nichols was expected to marry a wealthy man with social connections. Her parents had a plan for Ruth, and she didn't want to disappoint them. Yet Nichols was also worried, asking herself an important question: Did she have a right to live her own life? Shortly after her eighteenth birthday, in early 1919, she got an idea of what that might feel like.

A flier named Eddie Stinson was in Atlantic City giving airplane rides, and Ruth's father wanted her to have one. Every fiber in Nichols's body told her not to fly in Stinson's open-cockpit, **single-propeller plane**. It seemed much too dangerous. She didn't even like roller coasters. But Nichols stood next to Stinson and smiled. She was five foot five and blue-eyed, wearing goggles and a helmet pressed down over her brown hair. She was going.

The plane took off and Stinson began to laugh, flipping his plane upside down to impress the girl on board. Nichols—eyes shut, stomach churning—was not amused. But she survived the flight. And by the end of it, surprisingly, her fear was gone. "I felt," she said later, "as if my soul were completely freed from my earthly body."

Just a few months later, emboldened by her moment in the sky, Nichols left home against her father's wishes. She wasn't getting married; she was going to Wellesley College, an elite school for women near Boston. "College life," she told her mother, writing home that fall, "is simply great!" There were costume parties to attend, lazy days spent swimming at a nearby lake, and joyful nights singing school songs in the moonlight. It was everything she wanted, and Nichols told her parents about all of it in letters she sent home, signing them with love: "Devotedly, Ruth."

———

Her parents weren't giving up just yet. After Nichols's second year at college, her mother and father pressured her to walk away from school. The offer: a winter in Miami. The goal: "to become a lady." This time, Nichols listened—for a while. That winter, she agreed to go to all the dances, theater parties, and Junior League activities that her mother scheduled for her. But she also wanted to use the time to learn how to fly, asking an instructor named Harry Rogers for help.

"How much are flying lessons, Captain Rogers?" she asked him one day near his **seaplane** on the water in Miami.

"They come high," he replied. "Sixty dollars an hour."

It was the sort of money that made flying impossible for most people. But not for the daughter of wealthy Erickson Nichols. Ruth was almost twenty-one now and agreed on the spot to pay Rogers five hundred dollars for his services—a decision that surely got the young pilot's attention.

Rogers was not like Nichols's college professors—not at all. In their lessons, Rogers yelled at her. "For Pete's sake," he'd tell Nichols when she was flying, "don't ask me why! Do it because I tell you!" Other times, he just insulted her, calling her "dumb," "the dumbest," a "nincompoop" flying at "numbskull speed."

But Nichols refused to give up, and soon she was flying on her own—solo in an airplane.

"I'm a flier now, Harry!" she told Rogers after her first solo flight.

"A flier, my eye," he snapped. "You've only just begun. But maybe," he added, "just maybe, you'll make it yet."

She returned to college in the fall of 1922, graduated in 1924, and then decided to sail around the world aboard an ocean liner that was attempting to become the largest ship ever to circle the Earth. This, Nichols thought, would be an exciting trip, and it was.

But soon she was torn between two worlds: her parents' world in New York and the world she wanted to create for herself; the marriage that was expected of her and the adventures she wanted to pursue on her own. Increasingly, she was sure of only one thing: the next time she went around the world, she was going by airplane.

There was just one woman she'd have to beat.

Ruth Nichols's pilot license—signed by pioneer Orville Wright—was just the beginning for Nichols, who wanted to set records in the sky. *Courtesy of Jeff Nichols*

CHAPTER 3
AN EXTREMELY INTERESTING GIRL

Amelia Earhart was living in Los Angeles the first time she flew. It was the summer of 1920, and she was just a passenger that day, paying a small fee for the thrill of a brief flight. Six months later, it would be different. In January 1921, Earhart approached a female instructor at an airfield in Los Angeles with a question.

"I want to fly," she said. "Will you teach me?"

The instructor, Neta Snook, liked Earhart immediately—the direct way she spoke, how she walked around the airfield with a book tucked under her arm, and how she wore her hair. Quietly, at home, Earhart had been cutting it off one inch at a time so that her mother wouldn't notice the gradual change.

But paying for flight lessons with Snook wasn't going to be easy. Money was tight for the Earharts. They were renting out rooms inside their home on Fourth Street in Los Angeles to help cover expenses. Earhart didn't even have the money to pay Snook at first, buying lessons on credit. Then she made a decision that made things even harder: Earhart wanted a plane of her own. "I want to fly," she said, "whenever I can."

To make it happen, Earhart took a boring office job, sorting letters in a mailroom. She asked her sister, Muriel, if she owned anything that Amelia could sell. And then Amelia's mother stepped in to assist. In the end, they collected enough cash to buy Amelia a Kinner Airster—a two-seat, open-cockpit biplane, made right there in Los Angeles—for about two thousand dollars. It was light and fast. "All in all," Snook noted, "it was not a plane for a beginner."

Twice, she and Earhart crashed in it. Once, the cause was too little gasoline. Another time, they crashed on takeoff, smashing the propeller and landing gear but not injuring themselves. Earhart had cut off the ignition switch before they hit the ground, reducing the chance of an explosion. She'd also apparently brought makeup, which she began applying as soon as it was clear that they had survived the crash. "We have to look nice," Earhart told Snook, "when the reporters come."

The reporters *were* coming. The West Coast aviation press soon took note of Amelia Earhart, who was not just flying around on weekends but participating in air rodeos, the air shows of the time. Just as notable, as far as her sister was concerned, Earhart seemed to be falling in love—with a man named Sam Chapman. He was an engineer from Massachusetts who was renting one of the rooms in the Earharts' home. He was tall and redheaded, and, above all, he seemed understanding. Chapman stayed quiet while Earhart spoke to reporters and made bold predictions. The next time she went East, she said, it would be by plane, in her Airster. "A Lady's Plane as well as a Man's," said Kinner ads in Los Angeles. "Read what Miss Earhart has to say after flying a KINNER AIRSTER."

It was an ambitious plan for Earhart. But like most of her plans up until now, it didn't work out. All her life, Earhart had been on the move. As a girl, she had lived in five different states and attended six different high schools. Because of her parents' choices, bad luck, or impatience, she couldn't seem to stay in one place. Earhart, it seemed, was always leaving something behind.

Now, in 1924, she was on the move again. With her parents' marriage falling apart, she was leaving Los Angeles for the East Coast. But she wasn't going by plane, as promised. Her Airster had been sold. And her local fame was gone with it. All she had left from her time in California, really, was Chapman, her boyfriend, who was moving back East too.

They were soon living a short distance apart from each other, just north of Boston. Earhart was living with her mother and sister in Medford while Chapman moved in with his mother in seaside Marblehead. They were engaged now—that's how Chapman described it, anyway. Engaged and sure to marry. "In the near future," he vowed. Because they were happy. "Happy indeed,"

Chapman said. But Earhart was feeling something different, something closer to hopelessness.

It wasn't just about the move, or the plane she had sold, or the fame she had left behind in Los Angeles. It was sort of about everything. Earhart had dreamed of being a doctor, or an engineer, or a poet. She had dreamed of going to college, too. And she knew such dreams were possible for a young woman like her, if she worked hard. Earhart kept a scrapbook filled with newspaper clippings about important women making news. She cut out the stories and pasted them on the pages as motivation, perhaps, or proof that she could do anything.

But by the summer of 1926, none of those dreams had panned out. Earhart had dropped out of Columbia University in New York—twice. She couldn't go back, she told a friend, "owing to financial difficulties." And now here she was in Medford, twenty-nine years old and working as a tutor—yet another job that, for Earhart, wouldn't last long.

She could have married Chapman; all she had to do was say yes. But instead, she made a different choice.

On August 18, 1926, Earhart turned up on Boylston Street in Boston to register at the Women's Educational and Industrial Union or WEIU, a bureau that helped women find jobs. It was run by women, for women. She was case no. 49166—just another woman seeking work at the WEIU and willing to stretch the truth to get it.

Earhart lied about her age, saying she was only twenty-seven. She overstated her education, adding three semesters to her time at Columbia, and she made it appear as if she had attended just one high school—not six. Earhart was retelling her story to her liking. But even she was realistic about her job prospects. Gone were her dreams of medicine and engineering. Instead, Earhart told the WEIU, she would be happy to work as a hostess, a teacher, or "anything connected with an **aeronautical** concern."

The screener, or person who took down her information, at the WEIU was impressed with her. Earhart was five foot eight with dark blond hair, gray eyes, and a dignified air. She was well-read and smart, and the WEIU screener noted these details, scribbling comments about Earhart on her registration card:

"An extremely interesting girl—very unusual vocab—is a **philosopher**—wants to write—does write."

But one detail about Earhart stuck out most of all.

"Holds a sky pilot's license?"

It was a question, not a statement. But it didn't matter. There was no job for Earhart in aviation, nothing connected with "an aeronautical concern." The WEIU placed her at Denison House, a settlement home in Boston's Chinatown that focused on helping new immigrants. She was going to be a social worker.

Outside Denison House, the streets of Chinatown bustled with life. The neighborhood was filled with Chinese-goods stores and Syrian restaurants, rug dealers selling carpets and crowded streetcars rumbling by on elevated tracks, churning up the dust of the city—a city that had no hold over Earhart. All she needed was a chance, and she'd be gone. "When I leave Boston," she told a friend, "I think I'll never go back."

CHAPTER 4
THE FORTUNE OF THE AIR

*I*t began as a dare of sorts, announced to the public on May 22, 1919.

"Gentlemen," it said. "As a stimulus to the courageous aviators, I desire to offer . . . a prize of $25,000 to the first aviator of any **allied** country crossing the Atlantic, in one flight, from Paris to New York or New York to Paris." It was signed "Yours very sincerely, Raymond Orteig."

Orteig was forty-nine, a Frenchman by birth—and not an aviator. He was a wealthy hotel owner. He owned two of them in New York City and seemed to have little in common with the heroic airmen who sometimes stayed in his hotels. He was short and stocky, a shepherd's son and an immigrant. At the age of twelve, he had left his small village in France and come by ship to the United States. Go to America, his grandmother had told him. "And see what you can do."

Orteig arrived in New York with hardly any money in his pocket. He was lucky to get a job at a restaurant and even luckier to move up: from waiter to general manager and, finally, to owner. By 1902, Orteig owned two hotels, luxurious establishments that helped make him rich. He assured aviators that he had the twenty-five grand to reward a successful **transatlantic** crossing. And in late 1926, pilots finally felt confident enough in their little planes to attempt a flight across the ocean for the Orteig Prize.

By accident, almost, Orteig's money was about to spark air fever and start a race that would end lives and launch careers, inspire men to fly and encourage a few women, too. "This flight," said one pilot, "will be one of the greatest feats ever performed by an airplane—if it succeeds."

━━

Everyone knew success was unlikely. To fly 3,600 miles across the ocean, pilots needed a plane large enough to carry up to seven tons of fuel but still light enough to get into the air. If they miscalculated, their heavy plane would crash on takeoff into power lines or trees, and everyone on board would die. "Dashed to pieces," the *New York Times* put it, "and burned alive."

If they had calculated correctly, they had a new problem: **navigating**, or determining which way to go. Over land, pilots could use maps and landmarks to help reach their destination. Over water, they had to rely on a compass, adjusting for winds that might be blowing them off course. Or more difficult: they had to operate a **sextant**, a tool first used by ship captains on the sea to determine one's location or position. Pilots couldn't leave the controls or even daydream for fear of losing airspeed, **altitude,** or both. Then darkness would set in over the ocean and they would get sleepy, nodding off while listening to the lullaby of the engine and nothing else. No other sound.

Anyone hoping to fly across the ocean—anyone chasing the Orteig Prize—would have to avoid these dangers and many others. Weather. Engine trouble. Pilot error. And they would have to do it for a long time. A flight across the ocean in 1926 could last thirty-two hours. Almost a day and a half inside the small cockpit of a small plane, over a massive ocean—lots of time for things to go wrong. And still, pilots went. René Fonck was first.

=====

He was a Frenchman, like Orteig, known for shooting down 126 German planes during World War I. For him, Fonck said, the trip wasn't about money. It was about bringing France and the United States together. So Fonck decided to leave from New York's most famous airport: Roosevelt Field, on Long Island. Its clay runway was more than a mile long, and Fonck would need every inch of it to get his plane—a giant tri-motored S-35 Sikorsky—into the air.

On September 21, 1926, the great flier appeared at dawn at Roosevelt Field dressed in a blue uniform and waving to a large crowd near the runway. He climbed aboard his silver plane with three crew members. Then, just before takeoff, he accepted a gift, courtesy of Orteig: a box of French pastries. He jokingly tested their weight before placing them inside the overloaded plane. Finally, with a salute, he said goodbye to America.

Fonck's airship—weighing fourteen tons—rumbled down the runway like an elephant with wings. Too heavy. It hit forty miles an hour, then sixty—then a problem. One of the wheels on the landing gear broke and slammed into the plane's left **rudder**. Fonck did everything he could to avoid hitting the crowd. But there was no way to avoid crashing. The plane slammed into a ditch at the end of the runway and burst into flames. Two crew members died, and Fonck was lucky not to be one of them. He crawled through the wreckage, dodging the fire. Then, with a bloody forehead, he watched his plane burn for more than an hour.

What happened, he said, could not have been helped. The crash, experts agreed, was "probably unavoidable." The plane was too heavy and the wheel had failed.

"It is," Fonck said, "the fortune of the air."

He still wanted to fly across the Atlantic, and others did too. But they did no better than Fonck. In April 1927, seven months after Fonck's failure in New York in, two American transatlantic planes crashed in final test flights, injuring or killing the airmen on board. Then, in early May, it was France's turn to try again. Heroic Frenchman Charles Nungesser and his expert navigator, François Coli, were going this time and they had a beautiful plane. It was thirty-two feet long and painted white: *L'Oiseau Blanc*, they called it—the *White Bird*. Many believed Nungesser and Coli would win Orteig's prize—for France. "Warmest congratulations," the

French minister of war told the men—*before* they had even arrived in New York. "Your **exploit** marks an unforgettable date in the history of French aviation."

On the morning of the departure, in Paris, a large crowd gathered, shouting "Bon voyage!" in the early-morning darkness. But Nungesser, calm and cool, just shrugged.

"We'll see you soon," he told the crowd.

He and Coli climbed into the cockpit, and soon the *White Bird* was buzzing down the runway. Twice, it got about ten feet into the air. And twice it came back down again, heavy with fuel. The crowd began to panic. The *White Bird* was running out of runway. Finally, with just fifty feet left, the plane limped into the air over Paris, rising into the gray light of the morning. After thirty minutes, Nungesser and Coli **disengaged** their landing gear and dropped it to the ground. They didn't need wheels anymore. In New York, they would land on the water, at the feet of the Statue of Liberty. The mayor was already waiting for them there. Others had planned a celebration at the Hotel Astor. Nungesser and Coli were expected by late afternoon on Monday, about thirty hours after leaving Paris. And in New York, people gathered, scanning the horizon for a speck of white—the *White Bird*.

No plane.

Fog moved in that Monday, and then rain. Still, the people stayed—ten thousand or more. They were excited to greet the brave pilots from France, to cheer them. But Nungesser and Coli weren't there.

By nightfall that day, many people had given up and gone home. But Nungesser's younger brother, Robert, refused to leave. He believed that Charles must have landed early—maybe in Newfoundland, the large island off the coast of North America. And back in Paris, his mother also believed her son was alive. "My prayers will save him," she said.

But Nungesser and Coli had vanished somewhere over the ocean. Exactly where or how or why, no one could ever say. Searchers never found the men or their famous plane. But reporters quickly found a new hero to shower with praise and glory. He had landed at Roosevelt Field in New York the very same week, a young airmail pilot from Minnesota: Charles Lindbergh.

⸻

Raymond Orteig was beginning to worry about the deaths of all these good men. And there was no reason to believe that Lindbergh's flight would end differently. Orteig had always imagined that the man who won his prize would have a crew, or at least a copilot. Yet here was Lindbergh, flying alone and traveling light.

"Are you only taking five sandwiches?" one reporter asked him.

"Yes," Lindbergh said. "That's enough. If I get to Paris, I won't need any more. And if I don't get to Paris, I won't need any more, either."

His plane, like Nungesser's, had just one engine. Also alarming: it was smaller than the *White Bird*. At least one aviation expert said Lindbergh's plane, the *Spirit of St. Louis*, was too small to get across the ocean. But just after midnight on May 20, 1927, Lindbergh made up his mind: he was going.

"Ready, Slim?" a mechanic asked him at the airfield.

"Ready," Lindbergh replied.

It was foggy at Roosevelt Field that morning, raining off and on—not ideal for flying. Even rolling down the runway was a problem. The landing gear sank into the soft clay. And as usual, Lindbergh's airship—heavy with gas—struggled to get into the sky. His takeoff frightened just about everyone who was watching: his fellow aviators and the crowd of five hundred people lined up along the runway. Finally, at the last possible moment, Lindbergh pushed the *Spirit of St. Louis* into the air.

He was aloft, but still not out of trouble. He was just fifty feet off the ground, so low that people at the end of the runway could see his face through the cockpit glass—and they thought Lindbergh looked old, suddenly aged by worry. The plane was headed straight into some trees. But Lindbergh found a break in the highest branches, cleared the treetops by just a few feet, and then disappeared into the morning mist.

Many began to wonder if they had seen Charles Lindbergh for the last time. At a boxing match that night at Yankee Stadium, the fight emcee asked the crowd to stand and pray for Lindbergh, and forty thousand fight fans did just that, removing their hats and turning their faces to the night sky. At that moment, Lindbergh was hundreds of miles out to sea, needing all the prayers he could get.

But the American press thought that Lindbergh's takeoff was "daring" and "magnificent." And Lindbergh wasn't reckless for having tried it. He was a "lion," reporters wrote. "Defeat and death stared him in the face," the *New York Times* declared the morning after Lindbergh's takeoff, "and he gazed at it unafraid."

When he touched down in Paris thirty-three hours later, nothing could hold back the crowds. A hundred thousand Parisians knocked down iron barriers around the runway and pushed past soldiers to greet Lindbergh. Back home, crowds gathered from Times Square in New York to Lindbergh's hometown of Little Falls, Minnesota, tossing their hats into the air. Lindbergh was quickly paraded through four cities on two continents: Paris and Cherbourg in France, Washington and New York in the United States. But realizing that this wasn't enough—that people wanted more— Lindbergh kept touring. In the summer and fall of 1927, he visited another ninety-two American cities in his famous plane for more parades, speeches, and parties.

The flier grew tired of all the attention. He complained, at times, about the parades or about the reporters following him everywhere. "Awaiting," one radioman said, "Lindbergh . . . Lindbergh is coming down the gangplank . . . Walking slowly . . . His hat in his hand . . . A darn nice boy."

He had won Orteig's prize and everything that came with it— the book deals, the movie offers, and fame. But Raymond Orteig, the man behind it all, felt like a winner too.

"I feel a lot lighter," Orteig said.

"Lighter by $25,000?" a friend joked.

Orteig shook him off. It wasn't about the money. "Lighter in the heart," he explained.

With Lindbergh's success, Orteig felt relieved. No one else would have to die trying to fly across the ocean to win his money. But Orteig and others hadn't counted on the female pilots.

They would do it for free.

This is congratulations after coming down from passing for my Dept. of Commerce license.

Louise

Louise McPhetridge was determined to fly airplanes and once she arrived in Oakland, Calif., in 1927, with D. C. Warren, left, she quickly made headlines. *Thaden Family Collection*

CHAPTER 5

THE FAIREST OF THE BRAVE AND THE BRAVEST OF THE FAIR

*L*ouise McPhetridge, Ruth Nichols, and Amelia Earhart heard about Lindbergh's flight the way everyone else did: on the radio, in the newspaper, or from friends sharing the exciting news.

McPhetridge had just arrived in Oakland, California, and was starting her new job selling Walter Beech's Travel Air planes. Earhart had only recently started doing social work at Denison House in Boston. By her own admission, she was barely flying anymore. And Ruth Nichols couldn't catch a break. In the spring of 1927, Nichols, twenty-six, was working in a bank on Forty-Second Street in New York, still living in her parents' house in Rye, and watching as a different Ruth—Ruth Elder, younger and Southern—made headlines.

Elder was going to be the first woman to fly the Atlantic, or she was going to die trying. Either way, Elder was about to prove two points: a woman with a good plane and a bold plan was impossible to ignore—and easy to criticize.

Ruth Elder arrived on Long Island that September, four months after Lindbergh's flight, with a style that was all her own. The Alabama native rarely appeared without a colorful scarf wrapped around her head, pinning back her hair. Her single-propeller airplane was equally eye-catching; it was a brilliant shade of orange. The color choice was purely practical. It would be easier to find the wreckage of an orange plane floating in the ocean. But Elder—and

Ruth Elder, wearing one of her signature "Ruth ribbons" around her head, took New York by storm in 1927. *Smithsonian National Air and Space Museum (NASM 92-702)*

her male copilot, a Floridian named George Haldeman—didn't plan on crashing her plane into the water on their transatlantic flight. It was too beautiful, too perfect, all the way down to the name painted on the side in large, cursive script: *American Girl*.

"Gas bought, runway ready, plane dandy, pilots OK," Elder told reporters in their first meeting at Roosevelt Field.

"What's your hurry?" one reporter asked.

"Do you only want to fly to Paris because you are a girl?" another said.

"Well, they've got pretty evening gowns there, I hear," Elder joked. Then, more seriously, she added, "I've never been to Europe. Might as well go this way. Get some clothes. Doll up a little. Come back by boat, taking it easy. No flying back for me."

The reporters wanted to know everything about her. Was she married? Was she afraid? Or would her family talk her out of making this dangerous ocean flight? No, she replied again and again. She claimed to have no husband and no fear, and said her family couldn't talk her out of doing anything. But reporters didn't believe her. They described her nose: "Perfectly powdered." They called her vain, and they pushed the twenty-five-year-old woman to admit that she couldn't be serious about flying across the ocean.

"What is this you're doing?" one reporter asked her. "Advertising a movie?"

"Oh, no," Elder said. "I'm really going to fly to Paris."

Didn't they understand? "I'm here to fly," she said. "Quickly."

Looking out at the reporters, Elder must have felt like she'd flown the *American Girl* to a different world. She was from Anniston, Alabama, one of seven children—not rich, not famous, and not telling the truth about her past. Elder had been married not only once, but twice. Her second husband was an electric-sign salesman named Lyle Womack. They lived together in Lakeland, Florida, where Ruth had a job answering phones in a dentist's office.

But some wealthy Floridians liked what they saw in her—the way she looked, the way she talked—and they came up with a business plan. They wanted to put Elder over the ocean with George Haldeman, a local pilot, flying with her. There was just one thing: Elder would have to say she had never been married. They were selling an idea—something exciting, and dazzling, and new—and the label couldn't say "Mrs. Lyle Womack," a wife answering phones in a dentist's office. It had to say "Ruth Elder."

Investors put up thirty-five thousand dollars to buy a plane, believing Elder was the right woman for the job. The main reason: she was beautiful, and they thought beauty would bring in cash. "The fairest of the brave," the press called her, "and the bravest of the fair." Elder would make it to Paris—or she wouldn't. She would live to tell the tale—or she would die. Either way, the reporters would get their story. Either way, the investors would make money. And either way, Elder thought, it was better than working at the dentist's office.

"I've lived for a while without amounting to a plugged nickel," she told one reporter after arriving in New York. "I want to do something that will make people notice me, that may give me an opportunity to get somewhere in the world."

"Is it worth risking your life?" the reporter asked.

"Yes, it is," she replied.

There was really only one way for Elder to blow the deal—by losing to another woman with a plane of her own. That woman was staring out at the ocean too, three hundred miles to the north.

———

The carnival rides at the Palace Arcade were usually the main attraction at Old Orchard Beach in Maine. But in the summer of 1927, the seaside resort was popular for a different reason: airplanes.

Pilots, hoping to fly across the ocean to Europe, were using the beach itself as a runway. For years, a pilot named Harry Jones had been working there, giving lessons. And soon, he had a new client: Frances Grayson.

"Please keep my plans fully confidential," Grayson told Jones. "You know how uncertain everything is in aviation." But as soon as possible, she hoped to come to Old Orchard Beach, take off from there, and beat Ruth Elder across the Atlantic Ocean. "We are not flying into the 'movies,'" Grayson said, brushing off critics of her own. She felt like they were flying into history. And like Elder, she was willing to die doing it. "I would rather give my life to something big and worthwhile," she said, "than to live longer and do less."

Reporters thought Grayson the opposite of Ruth Elder in

almost every way. Where Elder was southern and beautiful, Grayson was midwestern and plain—the "Flying Matron," newspapers called her. And where Elder was part of a new breed of American woman, Grayson was considered old. The Indiana native was thirty-five that summer, divorced, and working as a real estate agent in New York.

She was, at least, good at her job. By 1927, Grayson had sold two million dollars in property, opened her own office, and convinced a wealthy Danish woman to give her thirty-eight thousand dollars to buy a plane. It was to be a giant Sikorsky, the same kind of plane that Fonck had crashed in flames. But Grayson's airship, the S-36 Flying Boat, was new and totally different. It had both **pontoons** and wheels. In the air, it soared on massive wings, seventy-two feet from tip to tip. And on water, it floated. Grayson believed it could float for weeks if necessary, and she thought it the most beautiful machine she had ever seen. At the Sikorsky factory in New York, she stood in the shadows, day after day, watching the men build it and just waiting for her chance.

"Don't worry," Grayson told her family back home in Indiana. "I am not going to fail."

She was confident in who she was and where she was going.

"I am," she said, "a child of destiny."

———

Ruth Elder had no idea who *she* was anymore. By day two in New York, reporters were breaking the news that she had lied. Elder was currently married and had been before. They reported the facts and Elder cried, trying to explain herself.

"American women believe that a married girl's place is in the home and not in the cockpit of an airplane. I don't want to turn them against me," she said. "That is why I evaded direct answer to the first questions concerning my marriage."

She insisted that everything else they knew about her was true. "I'm no bluffer or faker," Elder said. She would still be the first woman to fly across the Atlantic. But aviation officials wouldn't let her take off for Europe. They didn't think a woman could make it—and Elder's financial supporters were beginning to wonder too.

Since Lindbergh's success in May, only one other plane had made it across the Atlantic. Every other plane attempting an ocean flight had failed. In August alone, sixteen people died in planes that were preparing to cross or actually crossing the sea.

The worst single event was a race from Oakland to Hawaii sponsored by a pineapple salesman named James Dole. Two planes in the Dole Air Race disappeared over the Pacific—five people dead. Then a third plane vanished trying to find the other two—two more people dead. Then three weeks later, just before Elder and Grayson arrived on Long Island, another plane was lost. This one was owned by one of America's most important men: William Randolph Hearst, publisher of the *New York Daily Mirror*. It took off from Old Orchard Beach in Maine, bound for

Italy, and then disappeared somewhere over the Atlantic—gone. By the time searchers found the plane, a week later, it was just pieces, wreckage—a chunk of wing, a few gas tanks, and a wheel.

That settled it: no more ocean flying. Too many good men, heroic men—"fine young men," Secretary of Commerce Herbert Hoover called them—had been lost, and too many funerals had been held. Many Americans thought that if the men couldn't do it, the women—Elder and Grayson—shouldn't even try. In early September, as news broke of the women's plans, officials in both Canada and the United States began pressuring lawmakers to ban, or **regulate**, ocean flights. Perhaps most significant, Charles Lindbergh himself spoke out against the women trying to make the trip. The man who had nearly crashed on takeoff at Roosevelt Field trying to win Orteig's money refused to comment on Elder or Grayson. But he seemed to question the women's plans. "It is rather useless to take off on flights involving great hazards unless there is some definite and worthy purpose in view," Lindbergh said. "I see no object in flying across hazardous ocean wastes unless there is a real purpose in mind."

By early October, the government made it even harder for the women. The U.S. Weather Bureau stopped supplying pilots with ocean-weather reports. Yet Elder refused to give up. She ignored her critics and passed every test that officials in New York forced on her. She passed their medical exam, and licensing exam, flying the *American Girl* solo in front of large crowds on Long Island.

Finally, after a month of delays, she and Haldeman got clearance to take off and awoke on the morning of October 11 to blue skies over Roosevelt Field. Elder was finished crying and tired of waiting. If she was going to beat Frances Grayson, the time to go was now.

"They shall not stop me," Elder said.

CHAPTER 6
THE LION'S CAGE

*T*he morning of Elder and Haldeman's departure, a team of mechanics pushed the *American Girl* to the long runway that made European flights possible.

There, a crew loaded the plane with everything Elder might need: five hundred and twenty gallons of gas, two rubber suits to keep Elder and Haldeman afloat, and a large knife to use to cut through the cockpit and escape the sinking plane if it crashed in the water. Finally, behind the pilots' seats, they tucked away a small basket filled with a few sandwiches.

With the basket on her arm, Elder looked like she was going on a picnic. She was wearing tan pants, a green-and-red sweater with socks to match, and her trademark rainbow-colored ribbon around her head—the "Ruth ribbon," girls in New York were calling it. She smiled for photographers with the ribbon in her hair. But inside, she was worried—worried about Frances Grayson. Grayson had flown to Old Orchard Beach in her Flying Boat the day before and might leave for Europe at any minute.

"Is she going?" Elder kept asking.

It was too windy most of the day for Haldeman and Elder to take off. Finally, just before sundown that night, they made the call: despite the gusty skies, they were going. They turned around to fly into the wind, as all planes do. Haldeman climbed into the cockpit, while Elder waved to the crowd that had gathered to see her off. Her signature hair ribbon was hidden beneath her helmet now. But her smile was still there as she said farewell.

"Goodbye, everybody."

Like everything else involving Elder in recent weeks, the take-off was a circus. Five hundred people were standing where the plane had been sitting all day. But since Haldeman had turned it around at the last minute to fly into the wind, the *American Girl* was now roaring toward the people and running out of runway. It looked like the *American Girl*, heavy with gas, might plow into the crowd.

Ruth Elder and George Haldeman, on Long Island, before their historic transatlantic flight attempt that October. *Photo by George Rinhart / Getty Images*

Police sounded the alarm, blowing whistles, and folks on the runway began to scatter. By one account, the *American Girl* had six hundred feet of runway left when its wheels left the ground. By another, it had only a hundred feet. Whatever it was, some people at the end of the runway ducked. The plane was so low—and so close—it felt like it could hit them in the head. Then they stopped, and they looked, and they cheered. Ruth Elder was up and away, flying into the night.

In the cockpit, Elder and Haldeman were thrilled, taking turns at the controls and singing to pass the time on the first night. But by morning—just fifteen hours into the flight and still less than halfway there—they began to have problems. The engine was using more gas than expected. Haldeman figured they had just enough fuel to get to Paris. Then, on the second night, the *American Girl* hit a violent storm, changing everything.

They could feel the plane failing now, hear the engine struggling. Ice was forming on the wings, making the plane hard to fly. The compass bounced around; they had to be off course now. Worst of all, the *American Girl* was leaking oil. With every hour, the oil pressure was falling.

Somehow, they outlasted the storm. But they couldn't outfly the oil problem. By the second morning of the flight—thirty-two hours after takeoff and at least eight hours away from Europe—they had to consider ditching. They brought their plane down low over a Dutch oil tanker. It was the first ship they had seen in more than twelve hours and their best shot now at survival.

How far are we from land? Elder asked in a message she tossed to the deck of the ship inside a cardboard box. *And which way?*

The plane circled while the sailors painted their reply on the deck.

True S 40 degrees west, Terceira, Azores 360 miles.

Elder and Haldeman hadn't even made it to the Azores, islands in the mid-Atlantic about 850 miles west of Portugal.

"We are going to land!" Haldeman shouted to the men on the deck of the ship as he made one final pass. "Pick us up!"

Haldeman zoomed away, looped back, and prepared to ditch while Elder grabbed the large knife they had packed. Her job: cutting a hole in the plane so they could get out and avoid drowning. As she pushed the knife into the plane's skin, Elder felt devastated. But she had no choice. They were done flying. It was time to swim.

The Dutch crew tossed each flier a line, reeled them in, and then watched as the *American Girl* burst into flames. It slipped beneath the waves and sank.

On the day that Elder left New York, Grayson didn't plan to go anywhere. She was naming her Flying Boat the *Dawn* and inviting the governor's wife, Dorothy Foss Brewster, to **christen** it in a naming ceremony on the beach in Maine. Brewster agreed to come. But on the beach, in front of the crowd, she urged Grayson not to make her flight. The governor's wife was worried about the danger—"the hazard of the enterprise," she said.

Grayson couldn't believe it. For weeks, like Elder, she had

been fighting off critics—people who questioned Grayson, in part, because she was a woman and, in part, because of her flight plan. A crew of men would be flying the plane—not Grayson herself. But Grayson fought back. The *Dawn* was a seaplane going from America to Denmark—with a woman on board. "This is a pioneer flight," she kept saying. It was a costly one too. Friends worried that Grayson was going broke to get across the ocean. Now, at the christening of her own plane, she was fighting off criticism again—from a woman, of all people. Worse still, she was losing to Ruth Elder. That night, just hours after the christening, Grayson learned that Elder had taken off, heading for Paris.

"I wish her Godspeed and all the success in the world," Grayson told a reporter in Maine, acting as if she didn't care. "There's glory enough for both."

Grayson was still making her flight. Twice in the next two days, she made plans to take off. And twice she canceled them due to storms. Still, Grayson felt good. In the storms, the **hull** of her floating plane hadn't sprung a single leak. Even better was the news she got later that week: Ruth Elder had failed. She was alive, but she had lost, ditching near the Azores. "Congratulations," Grayson wrote Elder from her hotel in Maine. "My prayers followed you."

Now it was her turn. Grayson had the plane and the crew to do it: pilot Wilmer "Bill" Stultz and navigator Brice "Goldy" Goldsborough. Stultz was an experienced airman, and Goldy had once helped Walter Beech win the 1926 Ford Reliability race. If anyone could chart Grayson to Denmark, it was Goldy. But he hardly got a chance to do his job. For the most part, they were stuck in Maine, due to mechanical problems and bad weather.

"Gray fog, gray clouds, all is gray," Grayson wrote one day while staring out the window. "And the lashing of the waves, the rain, the wind, remind me that it is almost November."

Frances Grayson—with the original crew of the *Dawn*, pilot Wilmer Stultz, left, and navigator Brice Goldsborough, right—hoped to beat Elder across the ocean."
Bettmann / Getty images

It was too cold now to fly the Atlantic, experts said. Snow was already falling in parts of Maine, making air travel dangerous at best. Frustrated about all the delays and failures, Grayson fired her pilot, Stultz, and returned to New York on the last day of October. But she wasn't giving up just yet, and by December she had a new plan. She'd leave from Roosevelt Field on Long Island two days before Christmas with a new pilot and a mostly new flight crew. Only one man was returning to fly with Grayson: her reliable navigator, Goldy.

They took off for Europe at sundown on December 23, heading north up the coast. The *Dawn* was expected to reach Newfoundland by morning, refuel there, and then head out to sea. But Grayson's famous plane never showed up in Newfoundland—or anywhere else. Instead, the *Dawn* disappeared.

Ships, planes, **navy destroyers**, and blimps led a search that soon covered a stretch of ocean almost three times the size of New Jersey. But they never found even a propeller blade from the *Dawn,* leaving people to wonder about what might have happened. Back in Indiana, Grayson's father canceled his Christmas plans. He was sure his daughter was alive—somewhere—awaiting rescue in her seaplane. "Built to float for two weeks," he said. Others believed she might be safe on land. At least two people in Newfoundland thought they heard the engines of the *Dawn* in the sky. And at least three others reported hearing the plane's last radio message.

Off Cape Cod: "Plane down."

In Bremen, Maine: "Can't last long."

In Newfoundland: "Where are we? Can you locate us?"

If any one of them was true, it was probably the one near Cape Cod. Sailors on board a British **schooner** eighteen miles off the Cape that night were sure they had heard a plane crashing. Outside the schooner, it was dark and snowing, making it hard to see anything. But the men all agreed on what they heard. It was the sound of an airplane engine, so close it was frightening. And then a loud splash. And then nothing but the sound of the sea.

Grayson and her crew had vanished, and officials quickly blamed Grayson for it. They had told her it was too cold to fly. They had told her not to go. "But she was very determined and overrode our objections," one U.S. official said. And soon the newspapers were blaming her too. They had celebrated the men, even the men who had failed. But they dismissed Grayson's flight as a daredevil stunt.

——

At first, Ruth Elder got better treatment. From the moment she reached dry land in Europe—safe, still beautiful, and now famous—people cheered her.

"There she is," Parisians shouted when they first saw her in late October.

"That's Ruth."

"*Vive l'American Girl.*"

She was fifteen days late, arriving in Paris by way of two boats and then a different plane from the one she set out in. But the crowd in Paris didn't seem to mind. In her transatlantic flight, she had fallen short, and Haldeman had done most of the flying. Yet Elder had still traveled 2,623 miles, the longest flight ever by a woman. There were parties to attend and speeches to give. Hollywood producers were offering Elder a total of four hundred thousand dollars for her story, for her time, for her face, for her name. President Calvin Coolidge greeted her in Washington when she returned to America, and people back in Anniston, Alabama, invited her home for "Ruth Elder Day."

"Oh, I don't know how to say it," Elder cried that December, looking out on the faces of her hometown. "But the people have just been wonderful."

Only they hadn't—not always. In Paris, the French made fun of her, calling Elder "the Happy Midinette" or "the American Midinette." Translation: "silly young girl." Elder's husband, Lyle Womack, seemed to agree. He said he expected Elder to stop flying, come home, and do what she did best: keep house. "Ace-high housekeeper," Womack said in one of the few compliments he paid his wife. "I'm very much in love with her," he said, "but I won't bask in her glory."

Within months, they were divorced. This too was probably Elder's fault, as far as the newspapers were concerned. She shouldn't have tried to fly the ocean. Even her hometown newspaper criticized the flight. "The nation will hope that Ruth Elder and other girls will stay on the ground hereafter," the *Anniston Star* wrote. "It is **folly** in anybody but a lion tamer to enter the lion's cage." Maybe most hurtful, important American women criticized Elder too. "She showed courage," said Winifred Sackville Stoner, founder of the League for Fostering Genius, a group focused on identifying the most intelligent children and raising them to be successful. "But what good did she do?" The nation, she said, would be better off if Elder did something else. "This afternoon, I am having as my guests at tea a number of high school girls who have won prizes for fast typing," Stoner said. "Any one of them in being a fast, accurate typist does far more for the community than does a dozen . . . Ruth Elders."

Elder was famous, and also completely lost. She was burdened by criticism that none of the men had faced either before or after they had tried to fly across the ocean.

Only one American female pilot, in fact, had publicly stood up for Elder, defending her against her many critics.

It was another Ruth—Ruth Nichols.

CHAPTER 7
FLYING SALESGIRLS

*T*he house in Rye felt gloomy to Ruth Nichols on that New Year's
Eve. She was almost twenty-seven. Not married or engaged, as
her parents wanted her to be, and not a real aviator. As the clock
ticked toward midnight, Nichols, alone in the big house, had to
admit she wasn't living her dreams. Instead, she was consumed
with worries—and a question.

How could she escape?

The recent newspaper stories about Ruth Elder and Frances
Grayson could not have helped Ruth Nichols's state of mind.
Unlike Grayson, Nichols was a licensed pilot. And unlike Elder,
she didn't require last-minute tests by New York officials. Nichols
had been flying for five years at that point. Why wasn't *she* flying across the ocean? Nichols had to wonder. Still, when given a
chance to criticize Elder, she didn't take it. "I would not call Miss
Elder foolhardy," Nichols told reporters.

As Nichols saw it, Ruth Elder was just a woman trying her

best—and Nichols had to support that. She was a woman trying her best too. But it was hard to stay positive that New Year's Eve. By the end of the night, Nichols was just sitting in front of a mirror, studying her face. She thought she looked old.

Just then, the telephone rang. It was her flight instructor, Harry Rogers, on the line, calling Nichols with an offer. He was about to make the first nonstop flight from New York to Miami in a seaplane. And Rogers knew the best way to get attention from the press: bring a woman on the flight.

"Want to come along?" Rogers asked Nichols.

"When do we start?" she replied.

Nichols headed to Rockaway Beach in Queens, New York, the next morning, New Year's Day 1928. She met Rogers there and got her first look at the airship that would make the trip: a single-engine Fairchild seaplane with silver pontoons. Sherman Fairchild, the plane builder, had big plans for his new machine, and Nichols was part of them. If she and Rogers made it to Miami, Nichols would prove Fairchild planes were safe.

Just before 8:00 a.m. on January 4, Nichols climbed into the cockpit of the plane. She hoped to keep her takeoff with Rogers a secret, then make a surprise landing on the water near the Royal Palm Hotel in Miami. But reporters found out, and they filled the next day's newspapers with details of the nonstop adventure, including the storm that Nichols and Rogers hit in Georgia—and survived—and the darkness they flew through in Florida and navigated. They had to follow bonfires burning on the ground just to find Miami. But the flight was smooth; perfect, even. Nichols and Rogers made the trip in almost exactly twelve hours, landing on the water that night and then stepping into the Royal Palm Hotel.

The crowd inside cheered Nichols—a rousing ovation—and reporters moved in, asking questions about her life. "Please," Nichols begged reporters, "let's not put in any more personal things." She wanted the story to be about flying—and about what women could do. With her flight to Miami, Nichols believed she had proven aviation was for both men and women alike. "I have always been interested in aviation," she said, "especially as a safe and interesting way to travel."

Sherman Fairchild, a plane builder, hired Nichols within the month. Her new title was "flying salesgirl," and Nichols seemed to like the attention that came with the job. She even wrote up a fact sheet about her life to give to reporters. She wanted them to know she wasn't just a **socialite**. She was a sportswoman who could do it all: play hockey and play piano, mush dog sleds and dance, ride motorcycles and golf. She claimed that she could even box. "Only a wee bit," Nichols said, "so please don't tell anyone." She wasn't, she said, "like a rooster."

Ruth Nichols was bigger than that. She was becoming a star.

———

Walter Beech, the Wichita aviator, knew he was smart. But after the craze over Ruth Elder and Frances Grayson in 1927, he must have felt like a genius for putting Louise McPhetridge in the Travel Air office in Oakland, California.

At sales stops across the state, McPhetridge's boss, D. C. Warren, did most of the flying at first. But the crowds turned out for McPhetridge. It made her feel silly at times. She was no aviator—yet. But she was learning to be a pilot. Sometimes, on their sales trips, Warren let her fly all by herself—and she'd get them back home to Oakland.

The men on the ground there liked her toughness, her **grit**. When there was work to be done on an engine, McPhetridge got dirty like the mechanics. Warren soon learned she could sell planes too. By early January 1928, only eight months after she had arrived in California, McPhetridge was the manager of the Travel Air office in Oakland.

The position made McPhetridge notable. Out of roughly twenty-nine million adult women in America in 1928, fewer than a dozen had pilot's licenses on file with the U.S. Department of Commerce—a tiny number. Female construction workers outnumbered female aviators. Female electricians did too. Indeed, there were more women working as lumbermen, policemen, newsboys, railroad foremen—fields so male-dominated that the job titles specified that gender—than there were women flying planes. Still, McPhetridge said, "I don't see anything strange about a woman selling airplanes. Women sell automobiles, real estate, and other things. Why can't they sell airplanes?"

In May that year, to help prove she belonged, McPhetridge got

America's 1,943rd flying license. Aviation pioneer Orville Wright himself signed the paperwork. And it helped get the attention of one man at the airfield in Oakland: plane builder Herbert von Thaden.

Thaden liked math and machines—airplanes most of all. Thaden learned to fly one when he was still just a teenager. Now, almost thirty years old, he was trying to build one—and this plane was going to be different from the wooden airships of the day. Thaden was using metal. A metal airplane would protect pilots in crashes, Thaden said, and last longer too. The future was clear, he believed. It was metal aircraft.

Herbert von Thaden, Louise's future husband, knew two things in the late 1920s: he wanted to build planes and he wanted to marry Louise. *Thaden Family Collection*

At the airport in Oakland, while McPhetridge was selling planes, Thaden set his mind to building one—and he knew what he wanted. He wanted engineers who were also pilots and a supply of a kind of metal called **duralumin**. Then he got to work, building a plane that was thirty-five feet long and fifty-three feet across the wings, with enough fuel capacity to fly for six hours. It was one of the first metal airplanes ever built in the American West, and everyone knew who made it. The name was painted across the tail: *Thaden Metal Aircraft*. Thaden himself called it the Argonaut, and not long after the first model was finished, in February 1928, he invited one person for a ride—Louise McPhetridge.

They seemed to be an odd couple, the young female pilot and the math-minded MIT grad. But Thaden didn't want to change McPhetridge. He didn't want her to stop flying, either. Thaden understood why McPhetridge loved flying, and McPhetridge understood why Thaden liked it too. He was always taking notes, working out the details. Because, in aviation, little details mattered. Pilots who missed something often ended up dead or, at the very least, at the hospital in Oakland—the Alameda Sanitarium. McPhetridge had seen it happen since arriving in Oakland. It was only a matter of time, perhaps, before she was headed to the sanitarium too.

In the summer of 1928, a plane she was flying stalled on takeoff. It was owned by a flying instructor named William "Sandy" Sanders. McPhetridge was flying his plane that day because Sanders wasn't feeling well. He needed someone to fly him from Alameda to Oakland, a short hop down the bay. McPhetridge volunteered for the job, and right away, on takeoff, there were problems with Sanders's plane. The engine quit—and that's when McPhetridge made her mistake. Instead of landing straight ahead on whatever ground she could find, she tried to turn back for the airport. With the turn, the plane lost speed, and down they went, spinning, crashing into the marsh.

McPhetridge suffered just minor injuries. Sanders was less lucky. He died the next day at the Alameda Sanitarium—and McPhetridge blamed herself for it. She had failed at a critical moment. A man had died as a result, and she never forgot how one little mistake could change everything.

That summer, Herb and Louise got married in Reno, Nevada. The couple had hoped to keep the wedding a secret until McPhetridge had a chance to go home to Arkansas. But people saw them in Reno, and the news soon made the West Coast newspapers: Louise McPhetridge was now Louise Thaden.

"Gosh," Herb joked in a letter he sent to Louise in Bentonville, "it's tough to be **notorious** like we are."

Oakland suddenly felt lonesome without her. "Don't stay too long," he begged her.

Louise promised him she wouldn't. She'd be back soon—and she always kept her promises.

CHAPTER 8
THE RIGHT SORT OF GIRL

*T*he publisher was looking for the "right sort of girl." She needed to be proper, but perhaps not too proper; pretty for photographs, but perhaps not too pretty. Finally, she needed to come from a good family—to have "good breeding," the publisher said—and, if possible, a pilot's license. This woman wouldn't be doing any flying, but it would look better if she could—and New York publisher George Palmer Putnam always liked things to look good. He claimed that the transatlantic flight he was secretly planning in the spring of 1928 was about science. But really, it was about a story that Putnam could sell. The famous publisher wanted to put the first woman over the ocean.

The name—Putnam—was one of the biggest in New York. George's grandfather had started publishing books in 1837. Nearly a hundred years later, that publishing house, G. P. Putnam's Sons, was one of the most famous in America. And his grandson George—or GPP, to friends—was at the center of it all. Putnam was a writer and an adventurer. He liked to travel and he loved the spotlight. As a friend once put it, trying to be nice, "George Palmer Putnam did not wear shadows well."

With America now interested in airplanes, Putnam wanted in, of course. In 1927, he published Charles Lindbergh's best-selling memoir for G. P. Putnam's Sons. It was one of the biggest books of the year. Then, in early 1928, Putnam heard a rumor that got him excited again.

"Pull your chair over," Putnam told businessman Hilton Howell Railey in a meeting in New York. Two airmen in Boston were secretly planning to fly a woman across the Atlantic, Putnam said. Railey worked in Boston; maybe he could check it out for Putnam.

Railey was game. He'd look into the rumor.

"What if it's true?" he asked. "What then?"

"If it's true," Putnam said, "we'll crash the gate. It'd be amusing to manage a stunt like that, wouldn't it? Find out all you can."

It didn't take Railey long. By midnight, in Boston, he had found his two airmen: a mechanic named Lou Gordon and a pilot whose name had filled newspapers the previous fall. It was Frances Grayson's original captain, Wilmer "Bill" Stultz. The two men confirmed the rumor. They were planning to fly the first woman across the ocean in a large tri-motored seaplane. There was just one problem. The woman with the plane—the wealthy Amy Guest—had backed out. Her family didn't want her making the dangerous trip. They needed a new girl now, "the right sort of girl," and Railey wanted to find her.

―――

Amelia Earhart's social-work job at Denison House was going well. By the spring of 1928, Earhart was living at Denison House on Tyler Street, impressing her bosses as well as the immigrants she was serving.

Many of them were struggling under new anti-immigration policies. At times, these policies broke up families, separated parents from their children, or forced people to pay smugglers to try to get across the border. "The stories of the hardships that are undergone by people who try to enter this country 'by the back door' are sometimes hard to believe," one U.S. official said at the time.

In her position at Denison House, Earhart tried to help. She organized English classes for new immigrants, visited their apartments in Boston's South End, shared home-cooked meals around their tables, and sometimes drove their sick children to the hospital in her fast yellow car. But she also refused to give up flying, finding ways to get into the air. Using her Los Angeles connections, she joined a group of men building an airport in nearby Quincy. Once, to advertise a Denison House carnival, she had borrowed a plane and tossed paper advertisements from the cockpit. A few months later, in the fall of 1927, she had flown again, but this time to prove a point.

A famous German woman, Thea Rasche, was performing air

stunts in Quincy for a large crowd when her plane went down. Rasche was uninjured. But Earhart didn't like the way it looked— for women in general. Wanting to make it clear that Rasche's crash had nothing to do with her being a woman, Earhart immediately found a plane at the airfield, took off, and completed Rasche's program. Reporters took note of the flier from Denison House while Earhart herself took note of other female aviators. The same month that Rasche crashed, Earhart wrote a letter to Ruth Nichols. "Because your picture has been appearing lately in Boston papers," Earhart told Nichols, "I make you the victim of an idea which has been simmering for some time."

She wanted to form an organization for female pilots. Nichols agreed it was a great idea, writing Earhart back and starting a friendship—and a rivalry—that would last for the rest of their lives. Nichols might have been famous in New York. But in Boston, there was no doubt about who was the best-known female aviator. It was the social worker on Tyler Street, pushing women to do more.

"Flying is still a man's game," Earhart said that spring. But she believed New England women might help change that—and soon. "I have hope," she said, "that this year will see many more women flying."

If Amy Guest's secret transatlantic seaplane had been sitting in New York or Wichita, George Putnam probably would have sent another man, not Railey, to learn about it. That man surely would have found a different woman to ride with Stultz and Gordon across the Atlantic. Thaden might have gotten the invite; Nichols might have too. But in Boston in 1928, if you were looking for a female aviator, there was only one call to make. "Call Denison House," a retired navy man told Railey, "and ask for Amelia Earhart."

The call came in during the afternoon rush at the settlement house as children ran around. Earhart declined to take it at first; she was too busy. But the man on the phone insisted it was important.

"You don't know me," he said. "But my name is Railey—Captain H. H. Railey." And his reason for calling quickly came into focus. "I might as well lay the cards on the table," Railey told Earhart that day. "Would you fly the Atlantic?"

—

The men behind the flight wanted to know everything about her. Most important, they wanted to know if Earhart would risk everything to fly across the ocean for no money while the men involved got paid—twenty thousand dollars for Stultz as captain and five thousand for Gordon as mechanic.

The first meeting in Boston was exciting; the second meeting in New York about ten days later with Putnam and others was, for Earhart, "a crisis." Mindful that the men were judging her—her grammar, her looks, everything—Earhart struggled. If she came off as too weak, she might be denied the trip. If she came off as too strong, too beautiful—or, in her words, "too fascinating"—she might lose on that count too. The men wouldn't want to be responsible for killing the second coming of Ruth Elder on yet another dangerous flight.

A woman today might face similar problems. Some employers still—wrongly—judge people based on their looks. And "strong" women, "fascinating" women still—wrongly—face criticism. But it was much harder to be a strong, fascinating woman in 1928, much harder to be someone like Amelia Earhart. So, faced with this challenge, Earhart made a decision. In her interviews in New York, she tried to be average.

Putnam kept Earhart waiting for an hour. When they finally sat down, he claimed to take no notice of her looks one way or the other. His lasting impression was that she didn't like him—and Earhart was pretty sure he didn't like her, either. At the end of the day, Putnam hurried her onto a train bound for Boston, hardly saying goodbye. "Didn't offer to pay my fare home, either," Earhart complained. Still, she felt good about her chances, or at least the answers she'd given to the men's questions, one of them most of all.

"Why do you want to fly the Atlantic?" one of the men had asked her.

Earhart just smiled.

"Why does a man ride a horse?" she replied.

She got the job. By agreement, Earhart was named the commander of Amy Guest's tri-motored seaplane—the *Friendship*. Stultz and Gordon were to report to Earhart. But over the next three weeks, she barely saw the plane or the men. Everything about the flight was to be secret. Earhart didn't even tell her mother, father, or sister what she was doing. Only a couple of people knew: Sam Chapman and her boss at Denison House, Marion Perkins. "I'll be back for summer school," Earhart promised Perkins.

At first, Earhart wasn't going anywhere. It was cold and wet in Boston for the next few weeks, and her plane—orange with golden wings, seventy-one feet across—had the usual problem. It couldn't get into the air. Twice, Stultz, Gordon, and Earhart tried to take off from the water in East Boston. And twice, they failed.

Other women were planning their own transatlantic flights now; sooner or later, one of them would succeed. Just as troubling, rumors were starting to spread about the secret plans in Boston. Putnam couldn't keep them out of the papers forever. The *Friendship* needed to get off the water—and get away. On the morning of June 3, Earhart and her crew tried again, following the usual routine: Waking at 3:30. Packing coffee and cocoa. Whispering on the water in the dark and then breaking the silence by starting the large engines of the *Friendship*.

Earhart sat on the floor of the plane, quiet, in a fur-lined flying suit and high-laced boots. Faced with the possibility of crashing and drowning—"It is," said one expert, "a 50–50 bet"—Earhart hadn't said goodbye to her loved ones. Instead, she wrote letters to be delivered if things went wrong. The letters—like Earhart herself—were direct and to the point. "Hooray for the last grand adventure!" she said in one note. "I wish I had won, but it was worthwhile, anyway."

From the beginning that morning, the flight was troubled. It took five tries for the plane to get off the water; it was too heavy, at five tons. Finally, the *Friendship* hit fifty miles an hour, enough speed to get airborne, rising above the harbor with the sun. Just then, the cabin door failed, bursting open. Gordon and Earhart nearly fell out the door and into the sea. They were able to close the door using string. But there was nothing they could do to avoid the problems they faced on their stop the next day in Newfoundland.

They landed there in a cove, planning to refuel in a tiny village called Trepassey. At most, they'd stay just one night. But loaded down with gas to get across the ocean, the plane was too heavy to get into the sky. And some days they couldn't even try, due to the weather. It was often foggy in Trepassey in spring and summer, a lesson that Earhart and her crew learned the hard way. "I do not know why they selected this port," one curious local said. But it was too late to change their minds. While the press pushed its way into Amelia's mother's home—"What in the world are you doing here?" Mrs. Earhart asked a reporter she found in an upstairs bed-room—Earhart waited in the village at the edge of nowhere.

"What is in store for us?" she wondered.

She lived on meals of canned rabbit—a common meal in Trepassey—weathered storm after storm, and waded through a sea of doubt. Two other women were planning to cross the ocean now; one of them had made it as far as Newfoundland too. "Our competitors are gaining on us," Earhart complained. But she was stuck there with her crew for two long, miserable weeks.

It was like Frances Grayson all over again, only without the tease of success. Despite multiple tries, Earhart's plane couldn't even get off the water. "All of us," she wrote, "are caged animals."

The official forecast on their thirteenth morning in Trepassey —"this trap," Earhart called it—was no better than any other. There were two storms out at sea, strong enough that one female rival waiting nearby in Newfoundland refused to fly. But Earhart was tired of waiting.

"We're going today," she said. The pilot, Stultz, wasn't pleased. He argued with Earhart while reporters watched. He predicted that if they had to land on the rough seas that day, the *Friendship* would crack up and sink. But Earhart, wearing pants and a short leather coat, tried to stay positive. "We have a dandy breeze behind us," she said, "and we are going in spite of everything."

In the cove near the little village, the plane rumbled across the water at full speed for about two miles, trying to hit that magic number: fifty miles an hour.

But it fell short. No lift.

They dumped gas and tried again, and then a third time. Still nothing.

It looked like that day's efforts to leave Trepassey would end like the others before it—with Earhart and her two male companions walking back to their rooms for yet another canned-rabbit dinner. But on the next pass, the *Friendship* briefly caught air.

Stultz turned the plane around, taxied to the far end of the harbor, and, at 12:18 p.m., hit the throttle one last time.

The plane gained speed slowly.

Forty miles an hour. Fifty-five. Sixty.

Finally, they eased off the water and into the air. The *Friendship* was flying for the first time in weeks.

CHAPTER 9

WHERE IS MISS EARHART NOW?

*E*arhart recorded the takeoff and everything that happened next in a journal. She had to sit on the floor, and it was cold inside the plane. Just forty-two degrees at times. While the men flew, she wrote down what she was seeing—her one and only job—writing about icebergs of clouds, mountains of fog, and Stultz at the controls, alert and ready. "Many hours to go." She noted the air pockets that tossed them around in the sky, the darkness over the ocean that night, and the left motor sputtering. "Sounds like water," Earhart wrote.

But mostly, she just sat there, wishing she knew how to operate the radio so she could at least help Stultz and Gordon. By dawn the next morning, the men needed all the assistance they could get. The left engine was still misfiring. They were running out of gas, and, worst of all, they were lost.

Back at Denison House, the immigrants were asking questions of Earhart's boss, Marion Perkins.

"Where is Miss Earhart now?"

"Is she still flying?"

"Is she coming back soon?"

Perkins had no way to know. Even Earhart and her crew didn't know where they were.

Then, just before nine o'clock that morning, they caught a break in the clouds and spotted something below. "Two boats!" Earhart wrote. But the ships were going north and south, not east and west, the way ships generally crossed the Atlantic. "Why?" Earhart wondered.

Stultz and Gordon didn't know either. Were they that hopelessly lost? Completely turned around? Where was Ireland? Should they ditch near a boat? Earhart—given a new job now—tried to get a note to one of the ships below, dropping a message like Ruth Elder once had. But Earhart's message, tossed from the plane in a bag weighted down with two oranges, missed the deck, splashing into the sea.

"Well," Stultz said, "that's out."

It was, Earhart thought, a "mess." Then, through the mist and the fog on the horizon, they saw it: land. It wasn't a shadow, and it wasn't Ireland, either. Somehow, the *Friendship* had missed that country entirely. They were flying over boat traffic in the Irish Sea, between Ireland and Great Britain, heading for the shores of Wales.

Stultz landed on the water about half a mile off the coast and taxied to a buoy, where he and Gordon fixed a line to keep the plane from floating away. For a long time then, they just sat there, unnoticed. There were no cheering crowds, no celebrations. These

At her homecoming in July 1928, Boston turned out to greet transatlantic heroine Amelia Earhart, center, and the men who flew her across the ocean, Wilmer Stultz, right, and Lou Gordon, left. *Courtesy of Purdue University Libraries, Karnes Archives and Special Collections*

would be, in some ways, the last quiet moments Amelia Earhart would ever have. By lunchtime, she was a global star with the full power of the George Putnam **publicity** machine at her back, ready to publish a book about her flight and setting up parades in her honor across America.

In Boston, two hundred and fifty thousand people lined the streets to welcome her home, and two thousand social workers, mostly women, crammed into a ballroom to greet her personally. They wanted to see her, touch her, even sing songs about her.

But the greatest celebration of them all, Earhart thought, was in Medford, with her mother and sister and Chapman in the crowd. They were a couple, Sam and Amelia, but not for long. She was leaving him behind, for reasons neither would ever reveal but that seemed clear to Earhart's sister. Chapman thought Earhart too strong, her sister believed, while Earhart thought Chapman too weak. Chapman would never marry, dying single and young, and Earhart would never again live in Boston or Medford, leaving New England behind as she'd once promised she would if ever given the chance.

She was moving to New York to spend the summer with George Putnam and his wife in Rye—coincidentally, the same town where

Ruth Nichols grew up—and writing the book that Putnam wanted. It was the story of a heroine who conquered the ocean like Lindbergh. Many Americans thought she even looked like Lindbergh. She was a modest young woman, an "all-right girl." "The best-known girl in America," newspapers called her. "A slender girl . . . a pink-faced girl." She was, as Putnam liked to say, "a little lady."

"What's the matter?" Hilton Railey asked Earhart at one point that summer amid the celebrations. "Aren't you excited?"

"Excited?" she replied. "No."

As Earhart saw it, she had achieved little with her *Friendship* flight. "I was just baggage," she told Railey. "Like a sack of potatoes."

She hadn't flown the plane. She hadn't charted the course. She had just sat there, adding weight to an already overloaded airship. "She might well have been replaced with two hours' gasoline supply," one male pilot complained.

Earhart was famous, yes. But famous for doing nothing—and she knew it. To Earhart's credit, however, she refused to be famous for just being flown across the ocean by men. As the world celebrated her with parades and parties, Earhart was already making plans—bigger plans. One day soon, Earhart was going to prove she was a real pilot.

PART II

CHAPTER 10
CITY OF DESTINY

*I*nside the Ambassador Hotel in Los Angeles, powerful men were getting ready to put on an airplane race. Nine days of air races, actually—with prizes and trophies, winners and losers, and stunts, lots of stunts to thrill the massive crowds.

The idea of racing airplanes wasn't new. Almost as soon as planes were flying, pilots were competing to see who was faster. By the 1920s, these competitions had a formal name: the National Air Races. One lucky city would be chosen to hold them every year. But the recent races had been small or poorly planned—or both.

With the 1928 races, several cities hoped to change all that. San Francisco, Atlanta, and Des Moines fought to stage the races. But in the end, organizers chose Los Angeles because of its promises. Los Angeles planned to double the crowds, triple the prizes, and serve up nine days of perfect weather on a brand-new airfield.

It was a lot to deliver. A job for a true showman and a salesman.

A job for a man named Cliff Henderson.

As a boy in rural Iowa, Henderson had learned how to sell, hustling with his older brother Phil to make money any way they could. Together, in the small town of Shenandoah, the Henderson brothers sold crops from the family garden, cow manure from their barn, or pelts from muskrats they trapped and skinned on their own. But he didn't stay in Iowa for long.

At the age of just seventeen, Cliff moved to Los Angeles by himself. He got a job at a drugstore and enrolled at Manual Arts High School, where he quickly became one of the most popular kids in school.

By graduation in 1916, Henderson felt like he had lived in Los Angeles his entire life, and he enrolled in the college of his dreams: the University of Southern California. But his time there didn't last long. When World War I broke out, he enlisted in the armed forces. He served as an ambulance driver in France and Germany, then transferred to the air service and learned to fly. When he finally returned to California at the end of the war, Henderson chose a different path. Instead of going back to college, he married his sweetheart, Helen, and opened a car dealership. He was doing what he loved most—selling—and he reunited with the man who helped him do it best: his brother Phil.

No one could match Henderson's unusual sales promotions at his car dealership near the beach in Santa Monica. He had purchased an old plane and was offering rides to customers. FREE

Cliff Henderson flew an airplane to help advertise his first business: a Nash automobile dealership in Santa Monica, Calif. *Courtesy of the Historical Society of Palm Desert*

AIRPLANE RIDE WITH EACH USED CAR, his signs promised. But the airplane rides, the sales, and the success soon came to an end for Henderson. By September 1927, Cliff Henderson Motors was at least twenty thousand dollars in debt. He was rethinking everything when he heard about a chance to promote something new: the 1928 National Air Races.

Henderson was desperate to get the job, and in the end, he did. Race organizers asked him to solve their biggest problem first.

Los Angeles—home of the 1928 air races—needed an airport.

———

The city was about four times smaller than it is today. But it was growing fast.

It already had eleven airplane runways, plus ten more in nearby towns. But like most airports in America in 1928, these fields were just dirt and grass, open pastures—with no lights, no water, no services at all. The Los Angeles City Council, the air-race committee, and Henderson were hoping to find a real airport for the growing city.

Henderson had his eye on Mines Field, a piece of farmland in Inglewood, about thirty-five minutes from downtown Los Angeles. He said they should hold the National Air Races at the field, a place later known worldwide as Los Angeles International Airport: LAX.

But if the officials wanted Los Angeles to be a truly great city, an air-minded town in an air-minded time—they needed to act now.

"Line up, gentlemen," Henderson told them, pushing the city to acquire Mines Field. "The opportunity is not only knocking on your door—it is crashing down your door. It is by far the greatest opportunity that has ever come to a small city in California. *Grasp it!*"

Henderson wanted to hold the 1928 air races in a bean and barley field, an airport initially called Mines Field and later known worldwide by three letters: LAX. *Courtesy of the Historical Society of Palm Desert*

Local officials agreed to hold the races in Inglewood. Henderson hustled to get the field ready in time, and the races were as big as he had promised. That September, he awarded a record two hundred thousand dollars in prizes. He was able to draw three hundred thousand paying fans, and at least another three hundred thousand watched for free on the streets of Inglewood. He overcame every obstacle, even the death of an army lieutenant who crashed during the first weekend of the races in front of thirty thousand frightened fans.

The showman's great show was missing only one thing, really: women. For the most part, in 1928, women just watched—from Cliff Henderson's grandstand or from the chairs that he borrowed from the church down the street or from one of his stages. There were dancing girls to greet the crowds, model girls to sell the latest aviation styles, and attractive girls on display on the arms of hero pilots or next to the silver trophies they hoped to win. But the women weren't in the air.

CHAPTER 11

IF THIS IS TO BE A DERBY

*T*he flying women kept their silence—and, at first, their distance from Henderson's air races, his spotlight, and his stage.

That September, Nichols planned to fly west in the cross-country, New York–to–Los Angeles derby that Henderson had organized as part of the air races. Then she would attend the Famous Fliers ball. But Harry Rogers was going to be doing the flying, not Nichols. And in the end, Rogers's plane never got off the ground in New York. There was to be no derby and no ball for Nichols.

Earhart fared better—at the start, at least. It had been a busy summer for her. She had left Denison House in Boston's Chinatown to live with Putnam and his wife in Rye. She had written the book Putnam wanted, finishing it by the end of August. Then, one week before Henderson's races in Los Angeles, she flew west with Putnam in her new plane, an open-cockpit model called an Avro Avian.

The flight was smooth until Pittsburgh. The landing there that evening on a grass field was almost a total disaster. Earhart's plane hit a rut or a ditch. The impact ripped away one wheel, shattered the propeller, and cracked a wing, standing the plane up on its nose. Earhart was lucky to escape injury—and get help. Putnam put a team of mechanics to work, fixing Earhart's busted plane.

Soon she was back in the sky, flying west. She made it all the way to California before the end of the air races—her first cross-country trip by plane. Yet once in Los Angeles, Earhart tried to avoid attention, refusing even to land at Mines Field. She was worried, it seemed, about all the people who would be watching.

She didn't feel like a real flier just yet.

"I am just an amateur," she said.

——

Up the California coast in Oakland at that very moment, Louise Thaden felt like an amateur too. Like Earhart, Thaden had received an official invite to the races—at least to watch or fly around to delight the crowds below. No racing. But it had been less than three weeks since Thaden had crashed in Alameda, killing her passenger, Sanders. She stayed away from the races—or at least stayed out of the newspapers.

As soon as she had recovered from her injuries, however, she began taking chances like never before. "I am not a good pilot," Thaden said around that time. But she added, "I hope to be."

In early October 1928, Thaden prepared to set the altitude record for a woman. At a time when pilots flew at low altitudes, believing higher air to be too thin, too dangerous, Thaden wanted to reach seventeen thousand feet and keep going. It was a record

Shortly after her marriage in 1928, Louise Thaden began setting female records, intent on becoming the best woman pilot in America. *Thaden Family Collection*

that would require, among other things, an oxygen tank. Thaden borrowed one from a nearby hospital.

"You must be very careful," an intern at the hospital told her.

If she didn't get enough oxygen at high altitudes, Thaden could pass out. But if she got too much, the same thing could happen. When Thaden pressed for details to learn how she could strike the right balance, the intern just looked at her.

"Well," he said, "that's hard to tell."

In early December, after weeks of preparation, she went anyway. With a crowd watching, she took off from the airport in Oakland, climbing into the sky above the bay in her open-cockpit Travel Air. Once aloft, she was almost too uncomfortable to think about anything. The fur-lined suit she was wearing was too warm for the low altitudes and not warm enough for the higher flying. The parachute straps cut into her shoulders, and the chute itself pushed her up in the seat. Sitting higher than usual, she had to be careful to keep her head down or she'd catch bursts of ice-cold air in the face. Meanwhile, her oxygen mask kept obstructing her vision. But, half sweating, half frozen, she rose above the fog, flying almost four miles into the sky. Her record: 20,260 feet. Thaden now wanted more. "All world's aviation records for women," she said, "should be held by American women pilots."

Four months later, in March 1929, she claimed her second record. She took off in Oakland and flew in the air over the city for more than twenty-two hours straight, almost five hours longer than any female pilot had ever stayed at the controls of a plane. "Well, I made it," she said upon landing. "But, gosh, I'm tired." Then,

An exhausted Thaden gets a hug from her mother-in-law after setting the female solo endurance record in 1929. *Thaden Family Collection*

in April, Thaden added still another record, this time for speed. Over a two-mile stretch in the sky above Oakland, she hit 175 miles per hour in her Travel Air and set a sustained record of 156 miles per hour—faster than any woman had ever flown. In each record-breaking flight, Thaden hadn't come close to beating the men's records, usually set by military pilots flying military planes. Still, that spring, the *San Francisco Examiner* called Thaden the "World's Leading Woman Flier." Herb would have loved to have seen it for himself. He was proud of Louise. But his metal Argonaut airplane had sold in California, a big success. Then, in February of that year, his company was sold—an even bigger development—moving Herb and the Thaden Metal Aircraft Company to Pittsburgh.

For two months, Herb and Louise lived apart from each other—with Herb in Pittsburgh building planes and Louise in Oakland flying them. But by April, with the speed record in hand, Louise had finally had enough. She headed east to join Herb at his new office near the Ohio River. Almost exactly two years after arriving on the West Coast, Thaden was finished selling planes at Travel Air. She claimed to be finished chasing records too. "No more of the sensational flying," she promised.

She hoped to set up a flight school in Pittsburgh and teach women to fly. There was only one thing that could delay her. Thaden wanted to compete in Cliff Henderson's air races.

———

Henderson was struggling that spring, torn between Los Angeles—his home—and Cleveland—the host city for the 1929 races. In February, he flew to Ohio to interview for the job of managing the 1929 races—a job that he was excited to get. But within weeks, his wife, Helen, died—of a quick and mysterious illness.

Henderson—only thirty-three and now a widower—was miserable without her, all alone in Cleveland. His new office there was empty and cold. He was starting all over again and dealing with all sorts of problems—including, most notably, the problem of the women.

Elizabeth Lippincott McQueen, a Beverly Hills socialite, was the first to begin making noise. At Henderson's races in 1928, McQueen had hosted a breakfast and announced she was forming a new group, for women only: the Women's International Association of Aeronautics, the WIAA. "Our objective," McQueen said before the breakfast, "is to interest women in aviation."

Now, in the spring of 1929, McQueen seemed to focus entirely on one goal. She wanted Henderson to approve an all-female transcontinental race, the first women's air race ever staged.

"You are no longer a local figure in this great cause," she told Henderson that spring. "Will you kindly consider a women's contest race to the Cleveland air races?"

McQueen was planning a true derby for them, from Clover Field in Santa Monica, California, to the dirt field that Henderson was helping to prepare in Cleveland. And, one by one, the women signed up. "I see no objection to having a race start at Clover Field or any of the Los Angeles airports," Earhart told McQueen. Thaden was also excited, signing up as soon as she reached her new home in Pittsburgh.

But race organizers—all men—soon came down against McQueen's plan. They doubted the women had the stamina to fly all the way from California to Ohio, a distance of two thousand miles. One man said a flight like this "would be too much of a task on the ladies." Henderson's boss, race chairman Floyd Logan, suggested a much shorter trip—from, say, Minnesota or Nebraska. This was a journey the women could handle. And the organizers also suggested one more insulting rule change: each woman had to fly with a man.

Thaden was furious. As she saw it, Henderson and the men were trying to turn the women's derby into a "pink tea affair"—a precious little race for precious little women flying their precious little planes.

"If this is to be a derby, let's have it one," Thaden said. "Otherwise, we will be the laughingstock of the aeronautical world."

Earhart agreed, and she was ready to throw the full weight of her famous name behind a bold plan. They'd **boycott** the women's derby. Not go at all. On June 11, Earhart made the announcement.

"If we can't fly the race and navigate our own course through the Rockies, I, for one, won't enter," Earhart announced. "None of us will enter, unless it is going to be a real sporting contest. How is a fellow going to earn his spurs," she added, "without at least trying to ride?"

It was national news and terrible press for Henderson, still grieving over the death of his wife and working away in Cleveland. There was no choice but to strike a compromise. Race organizers said the women could fly alone, without men, all the way from Santa Monica, like they wanted. Furthermore, they declared, each entrant had to be a real pilot with a hundred hours of experience. In exchange, the women had to agree to make stops and overnight stays along the way—fifteen stops in all.

The women agreed. It was probably the best offer they were going to get. Now Thaden just needed to find a plane for the derby, and an old friend back in Wichita had a lead on one. The man who had given Thaden her job selling coal told her that Walter Beech was building a new plane in his factory. "A very fast ship," Jack Turner told her, "and only one." She should ask Beech about it. "Probably," Turner said, "the company would loan it to you."

CHAPTER 12

THERE IS ONLY ONE CLEVELAND

*I*t was terribly hot when Thaden returned to Wichita that summer to ask about Walter Beech's "very fast ship." But Thaden had bigger worries. She kept thinking about the other women, her competition in the women's air derby. They were getting fast planes of their own in the summer of 1929 and hoping to win the ten thousand dollars in prize money.

Earhart was trading in her open-cockpit Avro Avian biplane for a Lockheed Vega, the plane preferred by men seeking speed.

Nichols, the daughter of Wall Street wealth, couldn't afford to buy a plane of her own at the moment. By the summer of 1929, Nichols was trying to set up "aviation country clubs" across the nation. She hoped they would one day be like golf clubs, but for plane owners. And in her push to get the job done, she was spending a lot of money.

But she was able to borrow a plane at no cost: an open-cockpit machine known as the Ken-Royce, made by Rearwin Airplanes in

Kansas City. The famous Ruth Elder had acquired a Wichita-built Swallow. Gladys O'Donnell, a mother of two children from Long Beach, California, was training hard too. And three other women flying Travel Airs were sure to compete: Blanche Noyes, an air-mail pilot's wife from Cleveland; Florence "Pancho" Barnes, a big-talking daredevil from California; and Marvel Crosson from San Diego.

Crosson was breaking Thaden's altitude record that spring and lying about her age. She was twenty-nine years old—not twenty-five like the papers reported. But one thing was certain: she was going to be hard to beat. "Marvel Crosson," one newspaper declared, "is a sure winner." Crosson certainly hoped so. "I have given up my life to prove that women are the best pilots in the world," she said.

Thaden picked up her Travel Air plane in Wichita some two weeks after Crosson. It was blue and yellow and flawed from the start. The engine leaked **toxic** gas—carbon monoxide—into the cockpit. The gas nearly killed Thaden on her test flight to Fort Worth, Texas. She landed there dizzy and confused. But Walter Beech fixed the problem by running a pipe into the cockpit. Thaden would have fresh air now—if the pipe worked. It was the best they could do, given the lack of time. Thaden finally landed in Los Angeles on August 13, five days before the race was to begin. She wasn't the last one to arrive, at least.

Nichols was still limping west in her borrowed Rearwin. She had to make three forced landings before even reaching the starting line of the women's derby. In the last of the three—caused by a leaking oil line and an overheating engine—Nichols had to walk for miles across the desert just to get help. And now, because of everything, she had missed the festivities that the other women had enjoyed that week: the breakfasts, the parties, and the photos for the press.

"Come on out here, Louise," Elder begged Thaden at one photo opportunity while holding a trophy in her hand. "Come on, Marvel."

Elder, a film star now, was comfortable in front of the cameras. Thaden, Crosson, and others shied away. But there was one party every woman was expected to attend: the Aviation Ball inside the La Monica ballroom.

On Saturday night, the eve of the races, Thaden and Earhart, Elder and Crosson, Noyes and O'Donnell, and all the rest—except Nichols—stepped into the La Monica. They eyed one another and then the place cards at their seats. The cards bore a simple message.

"There is only one Cleveland. Find it."

CHAPTER 13
BEWARE OF SABOTAGE

*T*he race began the next day in Santa Monica. The morning after the party at the La Monica ballroom, they headed to the starting line at Clover Field. Some twenty thousand fans were waiting for them there. Everyone wanted to see the women leave for their first stop—San Bernardino, about seventy-seven miles east of Santa Monica—including Hollywood stars, like actor, writer, and comedian Will Rogers.

Thaden was no stranger to crowds. But even she was nervous as she climbed into the open cockpit of her blue-and-yellow Travel Air and waited for her turn to take off. She and Earhart and the other women had asked for this moment, this chance to prove themselves. Now that it was here, they realized there was more at stake than just winning. All twenty of the female pilots needed to make it to Cleveland, or they'd be criticized—for failing.

"The men, you know, have been somewhat worried about such a long flight for us," Earhart said that week, "and they seem to have visions of us smashing up all over the countryside. So the thing for us to do is to prove their fears have been foolish."

Thaden agreed. The women needed to be perfect, she felt. "One hundred percent perfect," Thaden said. And, also, "unduly careful." "If the derby is run off without a mishap, it will be a big boost for aviation in general," she said. But the opposite was also true. "If there is a mishap, the derby will defeat itself."

Roughly 20,000 people watched the start of the National Women's Air Derby in Santa Monica in August 1929— the beginning of a historic, momentous, and fatal week that would make the women pilots famous. *Thaden Family Collection*

On the airfield now, Thaden began saying her goodbyes.

"Good luck, old girl," she told Crosson.

"See you later," she told Earhart.

Then, waiting in the cockpit, Thaden waved to Noyes, sitting in the Travel Air at her right. Noyes waved back, hit the throttle, and pushed her plane into the sky. It was 2:18 p.m., and Thaden was up next, waiting for the starter to drop his flag. When it fell, she gunned it, rising into the sky and banking east for San Bernardino.

It was a short trip, the first of fifteen stops over the next nine days. They were divided into two groups: light planes and—the main division—heavy ships. The times between each of the stops would be added up, with the winner being the pilot with the fastest total time across the 2,400-mile route. A woman making mistakes in the air would have to live with them and hope to overcome them later on in the race. But it would be hard. Even a small problem along the way—engine trouble or getting lost—could set a pilot back, forcing her to lose time that would be difficult to make up later.

Thaden had no such problems on day one, finishing in second place, twenty-nine seconds behind Barnes, and followed closely by O'Donnell, Crosson, Noyes, Nichols, and Elder. Earhart finished a distant eleventh. The problem for her was mechanical. On takeoff in Santa Monica, her starter switch had shorted out, forcing her to return to the field and make a quick fix before going on. Another competitor didn't take off at all. A third woman flew too far, landing several miles past San Bernardino. A fourth didn't fly far enough, landing fifty miles short of the town. All were effectively eliminated. And one woman pancaked her plane in San Bernardino, damaging it with a poor landing in front of five thousand fans.

Up until that moment, the race had been known by its official name: the National Women's Air Derby. But in newspapers across the country the next morning, reporters began calling it something else: the Powder Puff Derby.

A powder puff was a product that women used when applying

makeup. And the term was everywhere in 1929. There were salons called the Powder Puff, the Powder Puff Shop, and the Powder Puff Beauty Parlor, and now there was this race, the "Powder Puff Derby." Newspapers loved using this name. Will Rogers piled on too. In his national newspaper column, Rogers coined his own term for the race: "the she derby," he called it. "They are aviators," he said, "but they are still women."

The female pilots didn't appreciate the comments; they also didn't like that the air-race organizers in Cleveland kept changing the plans. The men now wanted the derby fliers to stop in yet another place: Calexico, California, on the Mexican border. Given the lateness of the notice and the poor conditions of the Calexico airstrip, the women were refusing to fly there. They argued that they should skip Calexico, stop in Yuma, Arizona, and then fly on to Phoenix as previously planned.

Race organizers in Cleveland weren't happy. They threatened to disqualify any woman who didn't follow their directions. But the women back in San Bernardino were more concerned about another development.

"Beware of sabotage."

The message arrived via telegram that day, raising all sorts of questions: Was someone intentionally trying to damage the women's planes? Was someone *trying* to make them fail? Or crash? The women believed they had proof of, at least, something.

One woman returned to her plane after dinner in San Bernardino and found every switch in the cockpit turned on, every throttle moved. "Gas, ignition, primer, everything," she reported. Worried now, all the women returned to the airfield to inspect their planes, watching over them until after midnight. By the morning of day two—tired after just four hours of sleep—the women seemed to be losing on every front.

The race organizers in Cleveland were forcing them to at least fly over Calexico before turning east for Yuma and Phoenix. Worse still, the alleged saboteurs had gone to work overnight—or so it seemed. Arriving at the airfield in San Bernardino before dawn, the women found problems with their planes that they could not explain. Ruth Elder's problem was most alarming: the ground crew had filled her oil tank with *gasoline,* not oil.

Even if it was an honest mistake, it was cause for concern—and questions. Yet the women still took off, starting at 6:00 a.m., swooping low over Calexico as directed, and stopping later that morning in Yuma. The sand there was so deep that the wheels on the women's planes dug in upon touchdown, bringing their machines to an abrupt halt. Thaden nearly flipped her plane on its nose and then watched the others roll in, cheering them on in the heat.

"Stall it in—stall it in, atta girl . . . Now hold that tail down. HOLD IT DOWN! . . . Oh, Lord. I hope they all make it."

Earhart was the one who didn't. Upon landing in the deep sand, her orange Lockheed lurched forward and bent its propeller—a problem not easily fixed in the desert.

"Anything I can do?" Thaden asked her, trying to offer support.

"Well," Earhart replied, "yes, there is."

She was having someone fly in a new propeller from Los Angeles in a rush. Maybe, Earhart said, the other women could wait until it arrived.

"Why, sure we will," Thaden told her.

It was beyond hot in Yuma. But waiting for Earhart seemed like the sporting thing to do, and the women were nothing if not good sports. Earhart was a prime example of that. Since her Lockheed had more room on board than most other planes in the race, she had volunteered to carry some of the other fliers' luggage. And once, over a town that she had visited the year before on her long flight west, Earhart circled low and wasted five minutes to greet people there from the sky.

Of course the women would wait for Earhart. It was after lunch when they finally took off for the next stop, Phoenix, and soon they were all bouncing around in **turbulence**, engines running hot. "Too hot," Thaden thought. She hit a bump so hard at one point that she nearly lost control of the plane. She began hearing sounds in her motor—"disturbing knocks," she called them—and she worried about slamming into the jagged rocks in the sand down below. But she was flying too fast to worry about it for long.

With the crowd at the airfield roaring—seven thousand people in all—Thaden's airplane appeared first on the horizon, beating Barnes, the overall leader, into Phoenix by about a minute. Then came the rest: third-place O'Donnell and fourth-place Nichols, fifth-place Noyes and sixth-place Earhart. By the end of the day, every pilot was accounted for except one. Marvel Crosson was late—no word from her—and, by dinner, Crosson was officially missing. Somewhere between Yuma and Phoenix, her plane had disappeared.

"Marvel Crosson is down in the mountains," a reporter told Thaden that night at a banquet for the women at their hotel in Phoenix.

"Serious?" Thaden replied.

It was, for now, just a rumor. All they had were the eyewitness accounts of a few ranchers and a child near the town of Wellton who all thought they'd seen a plane flying low along the Gila River. In the morning, taking off for their next stop, El Paso, the women still didn't know anything for sure. They would have to fly half the day before they finally learned the truth.

Marvel Crosson was dead.

CHAPTER 14
NO TIME TO STOP

The wreckage of Crosson's Travel Air—found along the Gila River—offered few clues about what caused the plane to crash. All experts could say for sure was this: she knew she was going down and had chosen the flat riverbed of the Gila to make a forced landing. But, coming in fast, Crosson overshot the riverbed and then pulled the ripcord on her parachute, attempting to bail out— just fifty feet off the ground.

There wasn't enough time for it to open. At midday, at exactly 12:16 and thirty seconds, just twenty minutes after leaving Yuma, Crosson hit the ground, breaking her neck, snapping bones in both legs, and shattering her wristwatch, now frozen in time.

Almost immediately, people began demanding an investigation into her crash and into the other problems that the women were reporting with their planes. Only fifteen out of the twenty fliers had reached Phoenix on day two. Of the five who didn't arrive, one was dead, one was running late, and the other three were delayed by suspicious problems. One woman claimed her plane must have been fueled with "dirty gasoline." Another woman reported broken **brace wires**, the wires that helped keep a plane's wings stable. "They snapped," she said, "as squarely as if they had been cut by pliers." And then there was Ruth Elder, with her oil tank full of gasoline. Even though mechanics cleaned out the tank, Elder's plane struggled on takeoff in San Bernardino, flying along in a cloud of blue vapor. "I must have lost 10 minutes," she said, "flying in circles."

Robert Holliday, the publisher of the *Santa Monica Evening Outlook*, asked Henderson to stop the race and investigate. But Henderson and the other men in Cleveland refused to stop anything. There was no evidence of sabotage, they reported. Authorities in California had looked into it and found nothing. The problem was either "unsafe" planes or inexperienced pilots. Just like Earhart and Thaden had predicted, some people were blaming the women themselves.

"Women are lacking in certain qualities that men possess," Oklahoma businessman Erle Halliburton announced as the women continued flying east. Halliburton—the president of a small airline and an oil company—demanded that the women stop flying. Clearly, he suggested, they weren't ready. Crosson's death had proven it. And at least some reporters agreed. "For the present," one reporter wrote after Crosson's death, "such races should be confined to men."

The women—still flying, through El Paso and onward—weren't listening.

"This is no time to stop," Earhart told a reporter.

They had endured too much to even think about stopping. Thaden had flown past Barnes into overall first place—followed by O'Donnell, Nichols, and Earhart—despite sandstorms and wild winds. Blanche Noyes had survived a fire that broke out in the luggage compartment of her plane. The cause: a mechanic's cigarette—a careless man. And Margaret Perry, another female flier, had flown for days with a fever before finally checking herself in to a hospital in Texas. She was terribly sick— with **typhoid fever**.

But such problems were typical of hard flying, of racing. Men were also known to struggle when trying to fly across the country. In one competition at Henderson's races in 1928, nine planes piloted by men had taken off from New York and only one had reached Los Angeles. The others had been forced down by storms, ice, engine trouble, or crashes. Yet Erle Halliburton said nothing about any of that.

"Who is this Halliburton?" Earhart wanted to know. "Who is he to pass judgment on our abilities?"

As far as she and the other women were concerned, he was a stupid man, a fool. The matter was settled in a way that Marvel Crosson would have appreciated. The women—dirty and tired, but together—were going to keep flying.

"Why, we are just getting under way," Earhart said. "And with the worst part of our trip behind us, it is simply straight sailing to Cleveland."

Wichita was waiting, when the women arrived on day six. Fans there were excited to welcome them—especially Louise Thaden. And Thaden felt pressure to deliver. She took off in Tulsa that day determined to beat the other women into Wichita in what she called "the daily battle for a few precious minutes."

"Atta baby," she told her plane, upon arriving just after 3:00 that afternoon. "You smelled home, didn't you?"

She took off her goggles, placed them on her forehead, and then waved to the crowd while the spectators—wild and shouting—waved back. She had won yet again, beating the next plane into Wichita by ten minutes, and extending her overall lead. With only three days to go before Cleveland, Thaden was now up forty minutes on second-place O'Donnell; an hour and seven minutes up on third-place Nichols; and one hour and twenty-two minutes ahead of the fourth-place Earhart.

Her parents were thrilled to see her. But perhaps not as thrilled as Walter Beech. In Thaden, he had found gold, a treasure of sorts. Now he was making a plan to win, as usual. The Wichita airman— the "Knight of the Air" locals called him—met Thaden at the hotel that night to offer her some advice.

"You keep on the way you've been going," Beech said, "and you'll win. Save the motor all you can," he added. "Forget about the laps. Just win the race."

The next day, in East St. Louis, four hundred miles away, both Noyes and Earhart finished ahead of Thaden, cutting time off her overall lead. Not good. With the finish line—Cleveland—close now, they all seemed to be getting more competitive. No lead was safe, not even Thaden's—and they knew it. If she crashed at this point, she'd lose, because there was no time to make up lost ground. If she had engine trouble, she could lose too, for the same reason. Finally, there was always the chance of getting turned around in the air, misreading a map, following the wrong railroad into the wrong town, or even landing at the wrong airfield. "Ask any pilot,"

Some of the competitors in the first-ever women's air derby, stopping in East St. Louis, Ill., in August 1929. From left to right: Mary Elizabeth von Mach, Jessie Miller, Gladys O'Donnell, Thea Rasche, Phoebe Omlie, Louise Thaden, Amelia Earhart, Blanche Noyes, Ruth Elder, and Vera Walker. *St. Louis University Libraries*

Thaden said, "and he will tell you it is a difficult task to fly almost across the United States without once becoming momentarily lost."

Thaden was tired enough that she knew anything could happen. She could easily get lost. But she was also excited to get to the next day's destination: Columbus, Ohio. Herb was coming over from Pittsburgh to meet her there.

The next morning, Thaden was fidgety in the cockpit, sweating in the summer heat. She was bound that day for Terre Haute, Indiana; Cincinnati, Ohio; and then finally Columbus. She was eager to see Herb, "my sweetheart," she said. Nothing was going to stop her now.

On the way to Terre Haute, she added three more minutes to her lead. And by the time she reached Cincinnati, Thaden had put another five minutes between her and second place. After lunch on the ground there, she asked around the airfield in Cincinnati for a little help.

"Which direction is Columbus?"

There weren't many landmarks between the two cities, and Thaden wanted to be sure she was going the right way as she took off at 4:30 p.m. But soon after getting airborne, she felt lost. There wasn't another plane in the sky. The other women—wherever they were—had apparently taken a different route. More alarming, Thaden couldn't find the railroad tracks that she was supposed to be following on the ground. On a hunch, believing the wind had blown her plane to the east, Thaden adjusted her course so she was flying a little to the west. Still, there was no sight of Columbus.

She searched the horizon for an airfield, breathing hard as her hands began to sweat. It had to be close—she was sure of it. "That airport has just got to be around here someplace," she thought.

And still no Columbus.

She thought of Herb on the ground, studied her compass in the cockpit, and kept flying until, finally, she saw it: a brown field with a concrete runway on the Ohio flatlands—Columbus. Thaden nosed down, gaining speed, and crossed the finish line. Still in first place. A "sure winner" now, reporters told her.

Thaden refused to believe any of this "sure winner" stuff. As she saw it, she wasn't beating O'Donnell, Nichols, and Earhart by much. "Take it easy," she told herself the next morning, getting ready to take off for Cleveland and remembering Beech's advice: "Save the motor all you can." The day was filled with surprises as usual. Elder got lost—again—arriving last in Cleveland. And Noyes surged into fourth place—a stunning development. But nothing was as shocking as what happened to Nichols that morning in Columbus.

On a test flight, just before taking off for Cleveland, Nichols smashed her Rearwin into a tractor on the edge of the runway. The plane flipped over, wheels over wings, and Nichols flipped over with it, inside the cockpit. She wasn't seriously injured, but Nichols couldn't believe it. She had been in third place for days, one step ahead of the great Amelia Earhart and in line to take home eight hundred and seventy-five dollars, as much as most women made in an entire year.

Now her borrowed plane was crushed—"a squashed beetle," Nichols called it. Earhart—not Nichols—would finish third, and instead of giving a victory speech in Cleveland, Nichols was hitching a ride just to make it to the finish line. She'd miss the end of the Women's Air Derby, the so-called Powder Puff Derby, and the crowning of its champion: Louise Thaden.

Cliff Henderson was among the first to welcome Thaden to the finish line in Cleveland in 1929. *Thaden Family Collection*

Thaden had hardly landed when Cliff Henderson, looking dapper in a shirt and tie, reached up, grabbed her hand, and led her to the microphone to speak.

"I'm awfully glad to be here," Thaden told the crowd of forty thousand. "It was a great race," she added. "I wish everybody could have won."

Officials draped a large horseshoe-shaped wreath over her plane. Photographers began shouting at Thaden, asking her to pose, to smile, to hold the wreath just so. And reporters moved in to ask her questions. They were fascinated with Thaden. She was "slim like a boy," one reporter wrote, and wearing a shirt that appeared to be a man's. "Perhaps it was one of her husband's," one person guessed. Had to be. Because Thaden was too "dainty" for it to be hers. "Like a little girl," one woman cried in the crowd. How had she won the race? And what was she going to do next? Reporters wanted to know.

"There's one thing left to be done about the race," Thaden said. "The cup that goes with first place is going to be inscribed 'Marvel Crosson' and sent to San Diego. Any of the other girls would have done that too—had they had the luck that enabled me to win."

Thaden even tried to argue that winning wasn't such a big deal.

"Oh, yes, it is," second-place O'Donnell corrected her later.

"It certainly is," fourth-place Noyes agreed.

By surviving, by making it to Cleveland, the women were real fliers now. They had proven they could compete. But some men still refused to believe it. Back in Oklahoma, Erle Halliburton was still blaming Crosson's death on her own stupidity. "If it hadn't been for her fear and confusion regarding the course," Halliburton said, "she would have been leading now." He called the rest of the female pilots a flying joke, essentially. Some newspaper columnists seemed to agree. Most hurtful, perhaps, the women didn't get public support from the most important man of all: Charles Lindbergh. When asked about the women's accomplishments in their first-ever air race—a chance for him to give the female fliers his blessing—Lindbergh declined to comment.

"Is aviation a woman's game?" one reporter asked him that week in Cleveland.

"I haven't anything to say about that," Lindbergh replied. "I'm sorry."

In all that week, Thaden collected $4,600 in winnings—more than four times what the average American woman earned in 1929. Many of the other women had fared well too. But all the money they had made, all the crowds that had cheered them, and all the miles they had traveled didn't feel like enough.

Near the end of Henderson's air races in Cleveland, the female fliers met under a clump of trees on the airfield to talk it over. Earhart was there; Thaden was too. They wanted to discuss the future.

They all agreed: it was time to organize.

CHAPTER 15
GOOD EGGS

Cliff Henderson was thrilled—with the women, with the races, with everything. The 1929 air races had been the biggest ever held—just like Henderson had promised—and, indeed, one of the largest sporting events in American history.

Six hundred thousand people attended. One hundred and twenty-five thousand fans came out on Labor Day alone. Such crowds would dwarf those at the World Series later that fall. Perhaps more important, people who saw the races—or read about them—were inspired. They wanted to fly.

By year's end, the number of people with pilot's licenses in the United States had nearly doubled, to almost 9,500. Another 12,000 people were in line, trying to get into flight schools. And to meet the demand, manufacturers built more planes in 1929 than they had in any previous year in American history. One reason why: the female fliers. "Without women," one pilot said, "there can be no future for aviation."

Still, many women felt powerless on American airfields—like

"decoration," one female aviator complained. It had been just nine years since American women had won the right to vote, and a lot of men were struggling to understand these new women. They complained about their short skirts and short hair, their divorces (too many) and their marriage vows (all wrong). At weddings, brides were no longer required to promise to "obey" their husbands. That bothered some men. It threatened them too. But nothing was more threatening than a woman who could fly an airplane—a machine that had been invented by men, for men. In late 1929, there were only 117 female pilots in America, and some men felt the need to criticize these women, to call them names.

Swanee Taylor, the announcer at Henderson's air races, had lots of names for them, actually. Around this time, he wrote an article for a national aviation magazine, calling female aviators "helpless" and "absolutely powerless," "dependent" and "timid."

"Oh, how she squeals and coos," Taylor wrote, belittling women everywhere. "You are always captain to these babies."

He made fun of talkative women, and confident women, and said there was only one kind of woman he liked: the "Good Egg," he called her. "She keeps her chin up and a smile in her eyes . . . There is nothing petty or catty about her."

Everybody, he said, loves a Good Egg.

———

The women knew the odds against them. They knew what men thought. And in late 1929, they met in New York to organize—not around a single air derby, like McQueen had done, but around a bigger issue. They wanted to form a club, they said, "for all licensed girl pilots."

The group at the first meeting, held inside an airplane hangar, was small. It included five racers from that summer's Powder Puff Derby, five mothers, three editors, and two teachers. Yet the women were able to sort out a few matters, including, most important, the name of the group they were forming. Earhart suggested that the number of replies they received—the total number of charter members—should determine the name of the club. When ninety-nine replies came in before Christmas, they had their name. They were the Ninety-Nines.

Among the charter members of the new group were three of the most powerful women of all: Earhart, Thaden, and Nichols. During the formation of the Ninety-Nines in New York, they stayed together at Nichols's home in Rye. One evening there, after dinner, Thaden and Earhart each bragged that they could outwrestle most boys in high school. Before the well-mannered Nichols had a chance to stop them, Thaden and Earhart were soon wrestling on the floor. Nichols refereed until it became clear that Thaden had no chance. Three straight times, Earhart won. "Her strength," Thaden said later, "was absolutely amazing."

But with her Powder Puff fame, Thaden, twenty-four, had become a celebrity in her own right. Not as famous as Earhart perhaps, but close. Fans wrote poems about her. A Pittsburgh department store launched an entire fashion line around her: Louise Thaden Sports Dresses. And Thaden herself was thriving, teaching women to fly at the new Penn School of Aviation. By January 1930, more than a dozen women were enrolled at the school, and Thaden's new friends—Earhart and Nichols—agreed to come to Pittsburgh to help her.

The three women—rivals in the air—were becoming friends on the ground, the only friends they all had, really. They began spending nights in one another's homes. They coined nicknames for one another too. Ruth Nichols became Rufus, and Amelia Earhart became simply A.E.—the nickname that Amelia's publisher, George Putnam, also used for her. Thaden and Earhart were growing especially close, with Thaden rushing out to greet her friend anytime she flew through Pittsburgh.

They were the only ones who could truly understand one another. Earhart, Nichols, and Thaden weren't just flying airplanes; they were pushing for equality—the right for a woman to have any job or do anything. Women had won the right to vote in 1920, sure. Now they wanted respect, real freedom. They were pushing for change—and they were doing it in a difficult time.

Rivals in the sky, Earhart, Nichols, and Thaden became friends on the ground, helping the female pilots organize against the men. *Thaden Family Collection*

The stock market had crashed months earlier, in October 1929. With the crash, businesses began to struggle. Employers laid off workers. And many people, both rich and poor, now were fighting to survive. They didn't have money for even basic items, like food or clothes. It was a time later known as the Great Depression—a decade of economic troubles that would affect everyone, including young airplane builders like Louise's husband, Herb Thaden.

Herb was worried. His metal airplane company needed every sale it could get. Not just because he needed money—or because he wanted to succeed.

But because Louise Thaden was secretly pregnant.

With the birth of her first child, a son, in 1930, Thaden quit racing—for a while. *Smithsonian National Air and Space Museum (NASM 9A14419–017B)*

For a while that spring, the pregnancy didn't change much for her. She taught her classes and traveled for talks. She even survived a mishap in Harrisburg, Pennsylvania. A gust of wind nearly toppled her plane upon landing there, scooping the right wing into the air, throwing the left wing toward the ground, and spinning the plane around. Witnesses said only two things had prevented a disaster:

sturdy landing gear and a good pilot—Thaden, then five months pregnant.

But soon, there was no hiding the baby anymore. Thaden had to quit her job at the flight school. Employers at the time didn't like pregnant women working—especially a woman in aviation, a field dominated by men. Many men thought pregnant women were too delicate to work. Like it or not, Louise Thaden was forced to spend the summer at home, on the ground.

"Gosh, I'm anxious to fly," she said. "My hand itches something awful."

The baby came early, at least, arriving at the end of July. And the blue-eyed boy—six pounds and eleven ounces—was so beautiful, so perfect, that he changed everything for Thaden. Neither his wailing nor his crying bothered her.

"He's just impatient to fly," Thaden joked at the hospital. "That's all."

The baby boy, she thought, was just like his mother.

CHAPTER 16
MR. PUTNAM

As Thaden settled down in Pittsburgh in late 1929, Earhart was leading a completely different kind of life. She was thirty-two years old, eight years older than Thaden, but still unmarried— and free.

That fall, Earhart was darting back and forth between Los Angeles and New York. On the West Coast, she broke Thaden's speed record. On the East Coast, she wrote articles for *Cosmopolitan*, one of the country's most popular women's magazines. And no matter where she was, reporters followed, pestering Earhart and her mother back in Medford for news. "When and if reporters come to you," Earhart told her mother, "please refer them to Mr. Putnam."

George Putnam, the New York publisher, had something to say about almost everything Earhart did: the jobs she took, the speeches she gave, what she wore, even how she smiled. He was bossy by nature. And, as a result, at least a few of the other female fliers didn't like him.

But perhaps most telling about his character, Thaden wasn't fond of him. Earhart's friend worried about his honesty—or lack of it. She didn't like how Putnam seemed to take credit for Earhart's transatlantic flight. "You would think *he* had made the flight," Thaden said. Worst of all, she thought he looked down on the other flying women. "Everyone," Thaden said, "except Amelia."

Other female pilots doubted the motivations of George Putnam, right. But everyone agreed that he helped make Earhart famous. *Courtesy of Purdue University Libraries, Karnes Archives and Special Collections*

But even those who didn't like Putnam had to admit that he was effective. In choosing Earhart to fly across the Atlantic, Putnam had helped create a star, a woman who had many options at a time when most women had few. Earhart was writing articles, giving speeches, and making money to do what she loved most: flying.

Along the way, some reporters had difficult questions for her. They wanted to know what was going on between her and George Putnam. Putnam's wife had filed for divorce over the winter. Was Earhart going to marry Putnam?

Earhart, at first, denied everything. "If I were to become

engaged or married to anyone, I should certainly make no mystery of it," she said, brushing aside the question.

But on February 7, 1931, she married Putnam in a private five-minute ceremony at his mother's home in Noank, Connecticut—a ceremony that was witnessed by not a single member of her family. None of them got to see Amelia standing before the fireplace wearing a brown suit over a tan blouse—no bridal gown, no wedding party. Even Earhart herself seemed only half in, writing a letter to Putnam just before the ceremony. In it, she wrote about "my reluctance to marry, my feeling that I thereby shatter chances in work which means most to me." She went on to request that the two of them "not interfere with the other's work or play." Earhart ended with, "I must exact a cruel promise, and this is you will let me go in a year if we find no happiness together."

She signed it, simply, *A.E.* The bride was keeping her name.

CHAPTER 17
LAW OF FATE

*R*uth Nichols saw her chance. While Thaden was raising a baby and Earhart was getting married, Nichols was planning to shock the world. She was going to be the first woman to really fly across the Atlantic. Unlike Earhart, Nichols was going alone.

She had been thinking about it for at least four years, just waiting. She watched from her parents' home in Rye as Ruth Elder tried and failed, as Frances Grayson tried and vanished, and as her neighbor George Putnam put Earhart across the Atlantic in June 1928. Since then, only one other woman—a young widow named Beryl Hart—had tried to cross the ocean by plane. But like Earhart, Hart was just cargo; a military pilot was doing the flying. And like Grayson, Hart disappeared somewhere over the ocean, never to be seen again. Still, Nichols was determined to go, making a list of why it was so important for a woman to make a solo flight.

"OBJECT," she wrote, typing out her plans. "To show that a trans-Atlantic or Around-the-World Flight can be made commercially safe.

"TIME: To be stated as soon as the equipment can be purchased.

"CREW: Miss Nichols, as organizer and pilot of the ship."

She had begun seeking financial backers—individuals and companies to help pay for the flight—in January 1928, four months before George Putnam had ever heard of Amelia Earhart. But without a man like Putnam in her corner, Nichols couldn't find anyone to help her. Then Earhart's flight that June, her book about it three months later, and the stock-market crash of October 1929 all combined to make Nichols's ocean-flight proposal even less appealing. Businessmen, worried about the Depression, were looking to save money, not spend it. Most businessmen, that is.

In Cincinnati, radio **tycoon** Powel Crosley Jr. couldn't stop himself. He bought a plane, and a fast one—a red Lockheed. And Nichols just had to speak with him about his new plane. She could use it to break Earhart's speed record and perhaps fly across the ocean. Maybe Crosley would loan her his plane—his fast red plane.

In a stroke of luck, Crosley agreed. Suddenly, after years of waiting and watching, Nichols had a plane that could set records. And on November 19, 1930, she left Cincinnati, flying Crosley's Lockheed home to New York. It was a clear day, and Nichols felt good inside the cockpit—at least until she ran into the wall of fog in the Allegheny Mountains and opted to make a forced landing in a farmer's field.

It was a poor decision. On impact, Nichols crashed into a fence and drove the propeller into the ground. She was alive and uninjured, but the plane wasn't going anywhere now. Nichols was stuck in the tiny town of Manns Choice, Pennsylvania. She walked to the general store in town and called the only person she knew nearby: Louise Thaden, at home in Pittsburgh with her baby son, Bill.

"Where are you?" Thaden asked. "I'll come and get you."

Thaden stayed by Nichols's side until the Lockheed got fixed and back into the air that weekend. Then Thaden followed her friend by reading the newspapers. As Ruth Nichols was about to start setting records of her own.

In December 1930, Nichols set a transcontinental speed record, flying from New York to Los Angeles nine hours faster than any other woman had previously flown. Unsatisfied, Nichols turned around, flew back east, and set another record going in that direction too. In March 1931, she climbed back into the red Lockheed and set a new female altitude record: 28,743 feet. Then, a month later, in Detroit, she claimed one more record—speed—flying faster than both Earhart and Thaden. In the span of just five months, she had proven herself to be the fastest, bravest, and strongest female flier in America—and people knew it, sending letters to Rye to tell Nichols as much.

By April, she struggled to respond to all her mail. But Nichols took great care in replying to young people, especially young girls. June Thames, age eleven, in Brewton, Alabama, whose father had died when she was two, wanted Nichols to know everything about her. "My best sports are football, baseball, basketball, tennis, and golf." Frances Gunn, age thirteen, in Sanford, North Carolina, told Nichols she hoped to grow up to be just like her. "Many people think I'm a boy," she wrote, "but I'm a girl—a tomboy." Nellie Boich, age twelve, in Bisbee, Arizona, wrote Nichols to let her know she needed help. "Please write and tell me you will be my friend . . . P.S.: Don't forget to write."

Nichols didn't forget. She sent them autographs and advice. She was especially worried about young Nellie in Arizona. "If you are in any sort of trouble," Nichols told her, "I would suggest that you get in touch with a minister or a priest in your own town, as I am afraid I am too far away to be of any help."

Farther away than anyone even knew. In the spring of 1931, Crosley agreed to let Nichols fly his plane in one more challenge— the test that Nichols cherished most. She was going solo across the Atlantic.

Nichols believed that secrecy was the key to transatlantic success. But money was equally important. It was going to cost her twenty thousand dollars, or more, to get across the ocean—cash Nichols didn't have. So that March she began fundraising, asking at times a simple question: "Would you be willing to loan me $10,000 to attain my life-long dream? You know well, for how many years, I have wanted to make an Atlantic hop."

Important male pilots were supporting her. Clarence Chamberlin, the second man to ever fly across the Atlantic, was personally helping Nichols prepare in New Jersey. And Nichols herself was confident she would make it to Ireland or France. "There is no possibility of failure," she believed. The only thing that could stop her, she said, was fate—"the usual law of Fate."

It was a difficult time to be asking for money, with the Great Depression forcing millions of Americans out of work. People were panicking, even rioting, as they lost their jobs, their homes—everything—and moved into homeless shelters or **tent cities**. Yet, despite these problems, Nichols still raised the money she needed—proof that people believed she could get across the ocean.

Money began rolling in: $5,000 from Paramount Pictures; $5,000 from Columbia Broadcasting; $3,000 from her brother; $1,600 from one of Ruth Elder's former sponsors; and $1,000 from Crosley. Including a bank loan for $4,500, Nichols soon had enough cash in loans to make the trip possible. But in order to pay off the loans, Nichols needed to make money too. And to do this, she needed a man who could organize a historic flight, someone who had helped put a woman over the ocean before. The same person who, in fact, had discovered this woman himself, delivering her to George Putnam.

Nichols turned to Hilton Railey.

"Early in May," Nichols told Railey, "I am determined to attempt a flight from St. John's, Newfoundland, to Europe, with Paris as my actual objective." She wasn't seeking his advice. "My decision to make this flight is absolutely definite." She just wanted to hire him.

Railey didn't want the job. He resisted Nichols's proposal

By 1931, Nichols had everything she wanted: funding, a reliable plane, the *Akita*, and a chance to be the first woman to fly solo across the Atlantic Ocean. *Courtesy of the International Women's Air & Space Museum, Cleveland, Ohio*

for all the usual reasons: it was too dangerous, and she probably wouldn't make it.

"All right," Nichols said, finally getting angry. "Don't help me."

She understood what was happening here. "If I were a man, you'd help me. But because I'm a girl, you turn me down."

That was just wrong, she told him. But it didn't matter, because she was going no matter what. "I'll sell my car," she told him, "and everything I've got to make this flight possible." She was going across the ocean.

Railey finally agreed to help her—partly because they all stood to make money, *if* she made it. Railey estimated that Nichols could make $215,000 from the flight—between sponsorships and movie deals—and he quickly went to work. Railey secured Nichols a book deal, two magazine contracts, and an **endorsement** from a milk company. By April, Earhart, and just about everyone else in New York, knew what Nichols was planning. Her ocean flight was the city's worst-kept secret. But Railey was delighted to inform Nichols that Earhart—her friend and rival—was going nowhere. She couldn't beat Nichols across the ocean. "Definitely not to be considered," he said, allowing Nichols to focus on what mattered most: the flight itself.

That spring, Nichols met regularly with transatlantic flier Clarence Chamberlin, who was preparing Crosley's plane in New Jersey, and kept a list of everything she needed to bring with her.

She had maps of every state in New England, plus Newfoundland and Ireland. She had charts of the stars, the ocean, the moon, and British lighthouses. She knew which way the steamships were going, what they looked like, and what she would eat when she was hungry. She was packing three thermoses of coffee and soup, and also an emergency bag filled with six chocolate bars, two fishing lines and hooks, and a Bible. Nichols was packing for Paris, too. Amid her tools and equipment, she stashed away four hats, four dresses, three pairs of shoes, two different styles of bedroom slippers, and one special item: "Evening in Paris perfume." She made a neat little checkmark next to it on her master list and prepared to leave any day.

"I'll see you on the other side!" she told Railey.

CHAPTER 18
NO IN-BETWEEN

*R*ailey sailed to Europe on the last day of April. He wanted to be there to greet Nichols when she arrived in France and organize a grand welcome. By May 22, everything was in place. "Please advise Miss Nichols," Railey wrote home in a coded message, "that we are all set at London and Paris."

Back home, the Crosley plane was ready and more beautiful than ever. The Lockheed was no longer red but white with golden wings, and it had a new name dreamed up by Nichols painted across the nose: *Akita*. It was a word from the Dakota Native American tribe, Nichols said, that meant "to search, discover, or explore." But for the moment, she was doing none of the above. Test flights, bad weather, and then, on June 18, landing-gear problems were keeping her on the ground.

Across the ocean, Railey was growing impatient and, to be blunt, going broke. He had never intended to spend six weeks just sitting in Paris. Nichols needed to get to Paris, and soon, Railey thought. But the delays had given others time to try to convince

Nichols not to go at all. Even fellow members of the Ninety-Nines begged Nichols not to fly across the ocean.

"I guess the reason we don't want you to try is that we know there is no in-between," female pilot Mildred Morgan told her. "Go to it, if you feel that you must. But remember that if you do, and when you do, every girl flier in the country will be praying for you every minute of the way. None of us will sleep a wink until we know that you are safe across—and the most famous woman in the world."

On the morning of June 22, Nichols awoke in her room at the Commodore Hotel near the beach in Rockaway, Queens. As soon as she got word that the *Akita* was ready, its landing gear fixed, she reported to the airport in Brooklyn, arriving just after midday. It was hot and cloudy. But the weather was clear up the coast all the way to Saint John, New Brunswick, in Canada, where Nichols planned to spend the night.

Famous airmen—like Clarence Chamberlin, left, and Wiley Post, right—believed Nichols would succeed in her transatlantic attempt, seeing her off in New York. *Courtesy of Jeff Nichols*

"It is time that I got going," Nichols said.

She walked toward the *Akita*, calm and casual. Then Nichols climbed into the cockpit, tested the engine, hit the throttle, and pushed the plane down the runway and up into the sky.

The flight up the coast into Canada was easy, and by sundown Nichols saw the airfield in New Brunswick where she planned to stop for the night. It didn't look good. Instead of a wide field, it looked more like a small bowl, surrounded by trees. Believing she must have made a mistake, she checked her maps. But no, this was it. Despite years, months, and weeks of planning, she and her team had failed to properly investigate the very first stop on the journey. Now it was too late. With the sun in her eyes, and photographers waiting on the ground, Nichols decided to land.

She came in fast, at eighty miles an hour, half blinded by the sun, and missed her mark, touching down not at the start of the runway, but in the middle. Realizing now that she wouldn't have enough time to stop the plane before the runway ended, Nichols hit the throttle, trying to take off again. And for a moment, it looked like she would. With the *Akita*'s engine shrieking and its tires squealing, Nichols lifted the plane off the runway just before the landing strip came to an end. But there was not enough time. There was not enough space. The *Akita* was going to crash.

The rocks at the end of the runway ripped the plane apart in chunks. The engine broke up, the cockpit splintered, and the *Akita* stopped dead, jerking Nichols's body forward in her seat. People on the ground waited for an explosion; Nichols did too.

Get out, she told herself. *Get out.*

Wincing in pain, she climbed through the wreckage and fell to the ground—free, safe, and suddenly aware that she was not alone.

A photographer was already upon her, snapping pictures. Then half a dozen other men arrived. But they found no one to save, no fire to put out. Just an injured pilot standing there with a request for her would-be rescuers.

"**Wire**," she said, "for another plane."

———

It was, for Nichols, just wishful thinking. There was no other plane, no other chance, and no way she was going anywhere anytime soon. In the crash, she had broken at least two bones in her back. Doctors at a local hospital said she could expect to spend the next six to eight weeks in a plaster cast in bed. And she was lucky the news wasn't worse.

While she recovered from her injuries, Nichols had the *Akita* shipped by boat to Detroit, where maybe, with insurance money, she could pay to have it rebuilt. But gone was the book deal. Gone were the magazine contracts. Gone were the promises of big money. At this point, Nichols would be lucky just to pay off her loans.

In the crash, she'd lost everything.

CHAPTER 19
THE MAN IN THE MANSION

*T*hanks to his air races in Los Angeles and Cleveland, Cliff Henderson was getting rich. And he promised that the 1930 air races would be bigger than ever before. "The air race crowds will number at least 300,000 people," Henderson promised that summer, "and many optimists believe it may reach one million at this year's event."

The races in 1930 were going to be just north of Chicago at a new airfield in suburban Glenview. Henderson planned to feature Earhart, Nichols, Thaden, and the other women at the races there that summer. But the women didn't plan to participate at all because of new rules put in place to limit the female pilots. Under the rules, women couldn't race men. They couldn't race alone; a doctor and two U.S. Army planes would have to accompany them on any long-distance race. And their planes couldn't have engines as powerful as the men's.

"They naturally dislike the idea of going back to kindergarten," a race official said about the women. But the reason for the engine limitations was simple. "Without power restrictions," officials noted, "the prettiest flier would probably get the biggest plane of the best manufacturer, and if her luck and her flying skill held out she would probably reach Chicago first." They thought that plane makers would simply lend their planes to the most attractive women, who would enjoy an unfair advantage.

Henderson's work with the National Air Races made him a star in his own right, introducing him to movie stars, like actress Jean Harlow, at the air races in Los Angeles. *Courtesy of the Historical Society of Palm Desert*

Earhart, in particular, was furious. "Quite perturbed," Thaden told Nichols. On the one hand, the men were using the women to stir up excitement among fans—"selfishly exploiting us," Earhart said. And on the other hand, they were babying the women, acting like they were taking care of them—"we poor little women pilots," Thaden said. Soon Earhart, Thaden, Nichols, and the other Ninety-Nines made a decision. They wouldn't fly in the derby or in any other race in Chicago. They were out.

The races that August went off as scheduled, attracting a crowd of forty thousand people on the first day and an estimated four hundred thousand more over the next week. Here were heroic male aviators diving inside their red-winged planes. Here were the Lindberghs, Charles and Anne, escorted around the field by Henderson himself. Here were the races, including a new one: the Thompson Trophy race. In it, men whipped their planes around pylons—50-foot towers—placed across the field in a five-mile course, for a trophy made of marble, gold, and silver and a prize of ten thousand dollars, the largest sum ever awarded at an airplane race.

But the 1930 races made headlines mostly for one reason: flaming disasters. One pilot crashed into a cluster of other planes on the ground. A U.S. Navy captain fared no better. He was winning the first-ever Thompson Trophy race, cruising to victory around the pylons, when, for unknown reasons, the plane crashed, killing him. But the worst accident happened when a showboating airman flipped his plane upside down while crossing the finish line on day four of the races. The plane hit the ground and burst into flames, killing not only the pilot but a man at a concession stand and injuring a dozen other people.

It was like a bomb had fallen from the sky—not good for business. The races in Chicago barely made a profit. And the prospects for 1931, with the event returning to Cleveland, looked even worse. **Breadlines** were growing and tent cities were becoming more common by the day. Henderson needed help, a new idea, more money for a different race.

He needed Vincent Bendix.

Bendix's house in South Bend, Indiana, was so big that it had a name: Elm Court. The twelve-acre property featured an in-ground swimming pool—South Bend's first—as well as a small golf course. The house itself had three stories, thirty-four rooms, and fifteen fireplaces.

But it wasn't enough for Bendix, a South Bend businessman. Shortly after buying Elm Court in 1928, Bendix began making it bigger, better. He ripped out the swimming pool in the front of the house and replaced it with a new one out back. He added six more holes to the golf course. He built a bowling alley. He

Everything about manufacturing tycoon Vincent Bendix was larger than life: his mansion, his pocketbook–and the air race named after him, the Bendix Trophy race.
Courtesy of The History Museum, South Bend, Indiana

also changed the name of the enormous house. It was no longer Elm Court; it was Chateau Bendix.

Bendix's success as a businessman made it all possible. Even now, in the middle of the Great Depression, his business making car and plane parts made him important and wealthy.

Bendix, in short, was the kind of person Cliff Henderson needed. Henderson just had to meet him. Despite the crashes at the national air meet in Chicago, Henderson had a plan to boost interest in the races that involved even more danger: a transcontinentalspeeddash.Allheneededwassomeonetopayforit—Vincent Bendix, maybe.

"But how could I meet him," Henderson wondered, "and where?"

In early 1931, he got lucky. On a train ride from Chicago to New York, Henderson spotted Bendix in the club car and slid into the empty seat next to him to introduce himself.

"Mr. Bendix," Henderson said, "my name is Clifford Henderson and I've been trying to meet you for some months."

Henderson explained everything: that he was director of the National Air Races, that he was seeking a new sponsor for a grand new race, and that he wanted Bendix's money—and name—to make it happen. To Henderson, the Bendix name meant progress. "To me," Henderson told the manufacturer now, "the National Air Races mean the same thing."

Bendix was interested. But he didn't like Henderson's drawing of the trophy. A simple silver cup would never do for Vincent Bendix. He asked Henderson to draw something better, something bigger, and get back to him. The result was a trophy so large as to be ridiculous. The trophy was more like a statue, really, weighing almost a hundred pounds and standing nearly three feet tall, a prize of prizes for a race of races. Bendix loved it, approving this transcontinental race with a fifteen-thousand-dollar prize—the largest prize ever offered at the air races.

The Bendix Trophy stood more than three feet tall, weighed roughly 100 pounds, and initially came with a purse of $15,000—almost $250,000 in today's money. *Smithsonian National Air and Space Museum (NASM 83-2126)*

CHAPTER 20
GIVE A GIRL CREDIT

At the national meet in August 1931, two months after Nichols's crash in Canada, Bendix took center stage in Cleveland. He spoke via radio broadcast to the first Bendix race contestants sitting with their planes on the ground in Los Angeles.

"To you out there in California, at the starting line, two thousand miles away," he said, "I can almost hear your motors roaring as you'll be getting ready to give them the gun and this big field roars away in the dim hours of the night."

At dawn on the first Friday of September, the eight planes took off. One ran out of gas in Nebraska. Another went down in Indiana after an engine fire. But the other six made it to Ohio, with a green-and-yellow airship screaming in first.

"He's coming!" someone in the crowd shouted, spotting the plane on the horizon. "Doolittle's coming!"

Famous airman Jimmy Doolittle was racing in the Bendix in the name of science, he said. "If there's any reasonable project that will advance the science of aviation," Doolittle declared, "I'm ready for it, any time." But when he won the trophy—beating his rivals into Cleveland by a full hour and then hustling on to New York to set a transcontinental record the same day—Bendix and Henderson had the headlines they wanted.

<hr/>

Women often said they flew for the same reasons—for science— "furthering," Nichols said, "scientific aeronautical knowledge." They also believed they could defeat the men if given the chance, and now they had statistics to prove it.

With three years of air-race data to review, the Ninety-Nines pointed out that the women were, in some cases, flying faster than the men, recording higher average speeds, and, twice, even beating their male counterparts to the finish line. In a newsletter to their members, the Ninety-Nines said it was time for the men to "sit back and take notice." But Nichols would have been happy with just a little more respect. As she put it, "Give a girl credit."

In the summer of 1931, men made fun of her for crashing in Canada on her attempt to fly solo across the Atlantic.

"There, little girl, don't cry!" one wrote her while she was still in the hospital. "You aren't the first pilot ever to trade a Lockheed for a basket of chips and you won't be the last one . . . Only the next time you start transatlantic, please be frank and call your ship the *Flying Squirrel* if you intend to use it for climbing trees, scaling cliffs, and what have you."

Thaden tried to make her feel better.

"If it was in the cards for you not to go," she told Nichols, "perhaps it is better so, as something worse might have happened." But Nichols corrected Thaden. Her crash wasn't "in the cards," and it wasn't going to stop her from attempting another transatlantic flight. Within hours of her crash, in fact, Nichols was already planning to rebuild her plane for a second try. It could be fixed, if she could get the funding. "You can do anything," Nichols said, "if you can get the money."

Insurance helped cover the cost of replacing the fuselage of the plane. But in August, back in Rye, Nichols was still in her plaster cast and three thousand dollars short of the money she needed to finish repairing it. By the time the plane was ready, it was mid-September. Too cold over the ocean now; too stormy. And unlike Ruth Elder and Frances Grayson before her, Nichols was listening to the experts telling her to wait. She would fly the ocean in the spring.

The decision could not have been an easy one. Thanks to her crash, and the plane repairs that followed, Nichols was struggling like most Americans that fall. She was unable to pay her bills and requesting patience from those who had loaned her money.

That October, Nichols finally came up with an idea to at least keep herself in the news. She would use her rebuilt *Akita* to fly from Oakland to Cleveland or New York and set a female distance record. "The only record I do not hold at present," she told reporters on the ground at Thaden's old airfield in California. "To do it, I must fly 1,900 miles non-stop."

Two days later, near sundown, Nichols climbed into the

cockpit of the *Akita*. She was wearing a purple leather coat over a purple wool dress over a steel brace to support her injured back. It was going to be cold overnight, flying at fifteen thousand feet. Yet she wore no goggles, no helmet. This was, Nichols said, "just another flight," an easy trip, and the *Akita*'s perfect takeoff at 5:15 that evening certainly made it look that way.

Nichols rose above the bay with the moon behind her, darkness ahead, and the continent laid out before her beneath a blanket of stars. By one a.m., she was over Cheyenne, Wyoming, and by dawn, she was over Des Moines, Iowa, making good time. Then, inexplicably, in the daylight, Nichols got lost. She missed Chicago. Missed Cleveland. Wandered around in the sky for two hours and then stumbled on Louisville, Kentucky—way off course. Low on fuel and fearing bad weather in the Allegheny Mountains, where she had faced trouble before, Nichols opted to land in Kentucky— short of her goal but a record all the same. She had flown nearly two thousand miles, and the next day, she hoped to set yet another mark: a new speed record into New York.

The next morning, with a crowd gathered to see her take off, she climbed up onto the golden wing of her plane.

Moments later, with the plane engine in full roar and Nichols taxiing away from the crowd, a faulty valve on the *Akita* dumped fuel out of the right gas tank and onto the ground, splashing it everywhere. A spark ignited the river of fuel. And suddenly, the *Akita* was on fire. Nichols, moving quickly, scampered back out onto the wing and jumped to safety with the plane's engine still running. Yet there was no saving the airship. It burned for twenty minutes, the paint peeling off and the metal melting away.

For the second time in just four months, Nichols—already up to her eyes in debt—needed a new plane or significant repairs to fix this one. The estimated cost: ten thousand dollars—money that, once again, Nichols didn't have.

CHAPTER 21
GRUDGE FLIGHT

A melia Earhart saw her chance. With Ruth Nichols grounded and Louise Thaden refusing to fly the ocean—she thought it too dangerous with her baby son at home—Earhart was planning to shock the world. She, not Nichols, would be the first woman to fly across the Atlantic in full control of her own plane. Unlike in 1928, Earhart would not be flown by men. This time, she was going alone.

C. B. Allen—an aviation reporter who knew Earhart well—thought he understood why she would do it. By 1931, Earhart was a fading star, Allen believed, "gradually slipping out of the public eye." Quietly, Earhart—now president of the Ninety-Nines—set out to change that. She was planning a transatlantic trip that Allen called her "**grudge** flight." It looked like the kind of operation George Putnam would plan. In the months before she took off for Europe in May 1932, Earhart wrote a new book—to be published after the flight. In the meantime, she prepared in total secrecy. In the late winter and early spring of 1932, Earhart said almost nothing at all. She kept her silence while Nichols was all but screaming—for money, for help, for one more chance.

Between January and May, Nichols reached out to a long list of major corporations, begging for funding to make a second transatlantic flight.

It was no different from what Earhart was planning at the same moment, but the press gave Putnam's wife a pass while they attacked Nichols. "Flying to Paris—with What?" one magazine headline said. The story went on to suggest that Nichols had ruined Crosley's plane and wasted everyone's money trying to be the "Woman Lindbergh." But she would never get across the ocean, the article said, since she hadn't even been able to fly across the country the year before.

Nichols still hoped someone would sponsor her new flight. But one by one, major companies denied Nichols, sending rejection letters to her home. Nichols received the last rejection during the third week of May, the same week she and Earhart sat down for lunch in Rye. Nichols knew Earhart was up to something. Rumors of Earhart's transatlantic flight had leaked to the papers. But publicly, Putnam was still denying everything, and Earhart was too. At their lunch in Rye, Earhart revealed nothing to Nichols.

The same week, Earhart was equally secretive with Thaden, her good friend. She wrote Thaden, telling her where she could find important Ninety-Nines documents—"if anything happens to me." And she also told Thaden her dreams for the future. Specifically, Earhart said she hoped the Ninety-Nines would help women become leaders. But Earhart didn't say goodbye to her friend or even hint at what she was about to do.

Forty-eight hours later, Earhart's red Lockheed took off from New Jersey, heading north for Canada. Her secret was finally out and picked up by newspapers around the globe: Earhart was flying the Atlantic solo. Except initially, she wasn't flying the plane at all. Bernt Balchen—an adventurer with more ocean-flight experience than almost any man—would be at the controls of the Lockheed while Earhart rested. He was piloting the plane all the way to Newfoundland, some eleven hundred miles. There would be no Nichols-like failure before Earhart got out to sea, in part because Balchen would see to it—a detail not included in many stories about Earhart.

"Please don't forget to phone just the minute you get there, eh?" Putnam told his wife as he stood beside the plane in a conversation staged for the movie cameras.

"I will," Earhart said, her head sticking out of the cockpit.

With that, Putnam moved in for a kiss. Then Earhart smiled, looked at the camera, and, with a deep breath, retreated to the place where she was always most comfortable: the cockpit.

Now, in a scene that wasn't staged at all, Earhart walked to her red plane on the ground in Newfoundland. Balchen had taken her as far as he could. From here, Earhart would have to go alone. "To all my friends, both far and near," she announced, "let me say that you will hear from me in less than fifteen hours."

The goal was Paris, maybe beyond. And Earhart's takeoff in

Newfoundland that evening was easy—perfect, even. She turned east and pointed the nose of her Lockheed toward Ireland—eighteen hundred miles away—settling in for a long night of lonely flying. For the first couple of hours in the sky that night, Earhart felt good. The winds were calm and the weather fair. There was a lingering sunset at her back and a full moon rising over low clouds. She was flying at twelve thousand feet—and then, suddenly, she wasn't. The plane maintained altitude, but the altimeter in the cockpit failed. The gauge that was supposed to mark her altitude was broken. With no way for Earhart to know her altitude now, her plane bounced around, ran off course, and began picking up ice on the wings, a problem Ruth Elder had faced years before. Trying to find warmer air in the dark, Earhart flew low—dangerously close to the water. But exactly how close, Earhart couldn't say. Then, around midnight, new problems. Leaking fuel began dripping down her neck, and blue flames burned through a broken weld in an exhaust pipe—a frightening development. But with nowhere to land, Earhart kept going. By dawn, she knew Paris was out of the question. She was hoping for Ireland—if she could find it.

Back home in America, it was Saturday morning. Flight fans were turning on radios for updates, and Earhart's loved ones were sitting by their phones.

No news.

As morning dawned in New York, Putnam paced inside a hotel suite, waiting with Hilton Railey. It had been fourteen hours, and there was still no word from Earhart.

Finally, around nine thirty that morning, Putnam's phone rang.

"London calling," Railey said.

"Yes, yes," Putnam said into the phone, his eyes narrowing. Then, turning to Railey, he whispered the news: "A.E. is all right."

Her plane had landed in Northern Ireland in a farmer's field near the town of Londonderry. She was covered in oil, smelling of fuel, and almost deaf from the roar of the plane engine, but she was alive—a true transatlantic heroine this time.

"You have done an amazing thing," the mayor of Londonderry told Earhart a short time later, offering anything she wanted— even a fresh supply of gasoline, at no cost, so she could fly on to Paris. But Earhart was finished. For once in her life, she felt no need to go farther.

———

Whatever bitterness Nichols might have felt because a man, Balchen, flew Earhart to Newfoundland and whatever regrets she might have had because her own attempt had failed the year before, she kept to herself. She congratulated Earhart in a short, polite note. "You beat me to it for a second time," Nichols wrote Earhart, "but it was a splendid job."

Cliff Henderson thought so too. "Hurry back," he told Earhart. There was money to be made, speeches to be given, and that new book to write. Putnam would hustle it onto the shelves in just a month. Even Thaden was jealous. There was nothing she or any other woman could do in 1932 to top what Earhart had just accomplished.

In flying the ocean alone, Earhart had proven a point that each of them had been trying to make for years: Women belonged. They *should* belong. Even their male critics had to agree now. The women deserved to be included in any air race, over any distance, at any speed, in any plane. "This is the year," Henderson said, "for women's suffrage in aviation."

PART III

CHAPTER 22
SPETAKKEL

S he was younger than both Ruth Nichols and Amelia Earhart. Just twenty-seven in the summer of 1932 and lying about her age, saying she was twenty-five. Perhaps more important, Florence Klingensmith had no husband to look after her, like Earhart, and no child to raise, like Thaden. She was young and alone—and restless.

As Earhart returned to America by ocean liner in June 1932—finished with record-breaking flights for a while—Klingensmith felt like she was just getting started. She was willing to do almost anything to make a name for herself in the sky. Stunts, races, maybe even flying the ocean.

"I want to go," Klingensmith said, "if I possibly can."

It was like she was chasing the others—Earhart, Thaden, and Nichols—stalking the pack, coming from behind.

The Gundersons—Gustav and Flossie—had known early on that their daughter Florence was different from most kids in Kragnes

Township, a farming community in western Minnesota. She was filled with what the Old-World folks called *spetakkel*. "That's Norwegian," explained one local woman. "Means 'rambunctious.'" There was no containing Florence, not in the neat rows of desks in her elementary school, not on the family farm, and certainly not in high school. While the other girls at Moorhead High joined the debate team, the glee club, the class play, and the yearbook staff— the only activities available to female students—Florence found other hobbies. She impressed local boys with daring feats on the town ski jump and raced motorcycles—just for fun.

Perhaps not surprisingly, Florence didn't finish high school. She dropped out and began to drift. She chopped wood for a while in the northern forests of Minnesota and even herded sheep for a time in Montana. But soon she was back home again, living in Fargo, working at a dry cleaners called the Pantorium, and marrying one of her coworkers, Charles Klingensmith, in 1927.

Their marriage lasted less than two years. In fact, if there was a defining moment for Klingensmith in the summer of 1927, it wasn't her marriage but Charles Lindbergh's visit to Fargo. The town stopped everything for Lindbergh Day. Banks and stores closed. Thousands of people got up early and turned their eyes to the sky, straining to see Lindbergh's plane. Then, once he landed, they lined the streets to cheer him in a grand parade.

Klingensmith, just five foot four, pushed through the crowd to see him and waved to Lindbergh as his car rumbled past. When Lindbergh didn't wave back—as he often didn't, since he surely couldn't wave to every-one—Klingensmith was personally offended. She'd show him, she said, that he wasn't so important, that he wasn't the only one who could fly a plane. "Show him," she said, "a woman can handle one of these things, too."

Within months, Klingensmith enrolled in electrical school, the only woman among four hundred men, working her way up to mechanic's apprentice. She learned to fix engines and took flying lessons when she could. But she didn't have the

Florence Klingensmith—nervous before her first flight here, around 1928—soon emerged as the woman to beat in the sky. *Historical and Cultural Society of Clay County*

money to be a pilot herself. So Klingensmith took the only job that could get her into the sky on a regular basis: stunt girl. She began leaping from planes with a parachute on her back or standing on a wing high in the sky wearing only a bathing suit.

"It has been a hard ladder to climb," she admitted to another woman at one point. But in early 1929, it all paid off for Klingensmith. Businessmen in Fargo gave her three thousand dollars to help her buy her own plane—the *Miss Fargo*.

She was soon setting records, flying loops in the sky, and getting hired as a flight instructor in Minneapolis. She also won more than four thousand dollars at the 1931 air races and was prepared to win even more at the air meet in 1932, the first year of Cliff Henderson's "women's suffrage" races. These were the races where men and women would be equals.

But it didn't work out that way. Female pilots like Klingensmith couldn't get planes to compete with the men in 1932; manufacturers wouldn't help them. So, once again, they raced one another, with Klingensmith leading the way. That summer, she won the first-ever Amelia Earhart Trophy race in Cleveland, proving to reporters that she was for real, a real contender. "The men," one reporter said, "should be on guard against Florence Klingensmith."

All she needed was a faster plane.

When Klingensmith won the Amelia Earhart trophy at the 1932 air races in Cleveland, Earhart herself was there to congratulate her. *PhotoQuest / Getty Images*

CHAPTER 23
ANYTHING YOU WANT

*F*ifteen hundred miles east, on an airfield in Springfield, Massachusetts, a young inventor was building the exact sort of plane that Klingensmith needed.

His name was long: Zantford Delbert Granville. But his planes were almost absurdly short when compared to other airships. And they were fast, built to perform any stunt, flip, roll, or dive. He called them Gee Bees.

It was 1930 when Granville first entered the Gee Bee in the air races, choosing Lowell Bayles to be his pilot. Bayles was focused, intense, and small enough to fit into the cockpit of the little plane. Flying the Gee Bee, he finished second in a cross-country derby in 1930 and then returned a year later to do even better. At the air races in Cleveland in 1931, Bayles flew his fast Gee Bee to first place in the Thompson Trophy race. In all that year, Granville's Gee Bees brought home almost fourteen thousand dollars in winnings—and Granville knew exactly what he wanted to do with the money. He would use it to prepare the Gee Bee to set a new

Zantford Granville's fast and dangerous Gee Bee Super-Sportster could fly 300 mph, a marvel of its time—the perfect race plane for Klingensmith. *Courtesy of the Lyman & Merrie Wood Museum of Springfield History, Springfield, Massachusetts*

speed record. It seemed the Gee Bee could do anything. "Anything you want," Granville said. "The motor roars, but you feel no breeze."

But in early 1931, seven months before Bayles's success at the air races, the first Gee Bee fell from the sky. A well-known airmail pilot, Johnny Kytle, was flying in Atlanta, doing stunts at a low altitude, when he crashed and died.

It might have been easy to write off Kytle's death as accidental. But in the months to come, Gee Bee engines caught on fire. Gee Bee wings clipped pylons. Gee Bee planes, including both of Granville's entrants in the 1933 Bendix race, went down, resulting in the death of one of the pilots.

But the biggest loss—for Springfield, anyway—came in early December 1931. Bayles was attempting to break the speed record in Detroit. And on his second attempt, he seemed to have it. Witnesses watched in awe as his Gee Bee shot across the sky, like a shooting star on a string. Then, about a hundred and fifty feet from the ground, the plane suddenly dipped to the right and began to spin. Once around, twice around, three times—and down. On impact, the Gee Bee exploded into a sheet of fire, then rolled across the airfield for some four hundred feet. Bayles was dead, and witnesses on the ground knew what had happened. The right wing, made of wood and fabric, had snapped and broken.

Granville was forced to admit that the witnesses were right: the wing had failed because the wood inside was rotten—"very poor," he said. But the Gee Bee was soon returning to the sky, as difficult and as fast as ever. "To fly that plane," famous airman Jimmy Doolittle once said, "is exactly like the task of balancing an ice cream cone on the tip of one's finger."

In short, the aircraft was impossible—the perfect plane for Florence Klingensmith.

CHAPTER 24
SAY HELLO TO THE CROWD

Cliff Henderson personally invited Klingensmith to the 1933 air races in Chicago. "No doubt you have plans to participate," Henderson told Klingensmith. "If I can help you," Henderson added in a personal note, "let me know."

He and other air-race officials were finally making good on their promise to offer "women's suffrage" in the sky. That summer, both Amelia Earhart and Ruth Nichols had gotten approval to compete for the Bendix Trophy, hoping to beat four men from New York to Los Angeles—or, at least, each other. Neither did well. Nichols couldn't get her plane off the ground in New York at first, starting a day late, and Earhart was slowed by engine trouble. She fell hours off the pace in the Bendix and finally turned around near Amarillo, Texas, knowing she was, in her words, "hopelessly out of the race."

Klingensmith hoped to do better in Chicago, which was hosting both the air races and the World's Fair that Labor Day weekend. With both events happening at once, the city was preparing for nearly four hundred thousand visitors. And Henderson spared no detail to make sure they found his races in suburban Glenview. From his downtown office, he raised thirty-five thousand dollars in prize money and collected ten thousand dollars for the biggest event of the weekend: the Phillips Trophy race. It was open to both men and women who were willing to fly twelve laps around a course laid out with large pylons.

"We have a surprise for you," the race announcer told the crowd on Labor Day, the last day of the races. "Florence Klingensmith of Minneapolis has just filed her entry in the Phillips Trophy race."

In doing so, the announcer informed the crowd, she would be the first woman ever to compete against men in such an important pylon speed race. It was a decision she made, no doubt, based on her skill and confidence. But lots of women—Earhart, Thaden, Nichols, and others—had loads of each. Only Klingensmith had a plane that could compete with the men's. It was on loan, red and white and blazing fast.

It was a Gee Bee.

"Florence," the announcer said, turning to her, "step up to the microphone and say hello to the crowd."

—

Klingensmith glided past the men on the airfield, wearing light green riding pants, a brown jacket, and a beret.

All that weekend, the men had been teasing her, trying to find out if she was married. They also questioned whether she truly thought women were equals to men in aviation. Sure, women could fly, one reporter said. But none of them understood how an airplane worked. None of them had ever taken apart an engine.

"Ah, but I have," Klingensmith shot back. "Ask the men if I don't know all about planes. Ask them if I don't do all my own mechanical work. I learned planes from the ground up. I'm as good with a plane as any man."

Now, settling into the cockpit of the Gee Bee, she was going to prove it. As the engine roared to life, she could feel its strength—670 **horsepower**. And in no time at all, Klingensmith was in the air.

From the cockpit, she could see the three pylons laid out in a triangular course in the northwest corner of the field—far enough from the grandstand to keep the crowd safe but still close enough that the fans could watch everything. To make each turn, Klingensmith and the six male pilots competing against her had to fly 220 miles an hour. They had to go low, but not too low; tight, but not too tight; fast, but in control. It was the aviation equivalent of *spetakkel*—insanity—and there was no stopping it now. Just after six o'clock, they were off.

On the ground below, people watched as two male pilots quickly shot to the lead. At the end of the first lap, the crowd could finally see exactly where Klingensmith was; her red-and-white Gee Bee was challenging for third place, flying more than two hundred miles an hour and banking so hard that she tipped the plane vertically on its wing. A perfect turn, tight and fast around the pylon.

"Just look at that girl," the announcer said. "Did you ever see such a beautiful race?"

She was for real; the fans knew that now. She was surely going to make the money, as she had promised, taking third place or better. Then, at the home pylon on the eighth turn, a problem. The right wing—the same wing that had caused Bayles to crash—was **buckling** under the strain of the speed. Fabric ripped away in chunks, and with the air now whistling through the holes in her wing, Klingensmith turned off course, flying away from the crowd.

Everyone near the airfield was tracking the red plane now, hoping to see it turn back toward the field or to spot Klingensmith escaping with her parachute. But there was no turn and no parachute, either.

Instead, without warning, the Gee Bee crashed, nose-first, into the ground.

CHAPTER 25

HER LIFE FOR THE SHOW

*F*rom across Glenview, people came running. They found the plane in a small forest and pulled the limp body of the pilot from the cockpit.

They called for an ambulance, and, finding a pulse, medics hustled her to a nearby hospital. But doctors declared Florence Klingensmith dead on arrival, with a list of injuries that would have killed any pilot. A broken arm, two broken legs, a crushed chest, and a shattered skull. The cause of the crash should have been easy to determine. People had seen the fabric tearing away from the wing.

But local investigators—special air deputy **coroners** assigned to examine deaths due to plane crashes—weren't satisfied with that answer. Maybe, they suggested, Klingensmith herself had failed. Maybe she was overwhelmed. Maybe she had panicked. "I believe that she possibly fainted and leaned forward into that there stick," one deputy said, "throwing the plane into a dive."

In this scenario, the Gee Bee wasn't to blame. The crash was quite possibly pilot error. This seemed to make sense to the investigators. At the **inquest**—an official investigation into the cause of the death—they questioned everything about Klingensmith: her experience, her knowledge, even her body.

"Was this pilot examined before these races, as to her physical condition?" one coroner's investigator asked Cliff's brother Phil Henderson when he took the witness stand at Klingensmith's inquest.

"I do not believe that she was," Phil said. "I would not say positively, no."

The verdict, in the end, was simple. "A Gee Bee monoplane," the coroner concluded, "went into a nose dive apparently due to fabric tearing off the right wing." But reporters the next day seemed to blame Klingensmith, with the *Chicago Daily News* leading the charge. The paper reported that Klingensmith "wasn't well," that she lacked "stamina," and that she had died due to a "weakened condition."

Her funeral was well attended. But Cliff Henderson wasn't there. He was in Indiana dedicating an airport for his friend Vincent Bendix and then appearing at a party at Bendix's mansion for all the pilots who'd flown in for the affair.

Flying home to Chicago the next morning, three of Bendix's guests disappeared in a green airship over Lake Michigan. It would be five days before their bodies washed ashore. And that fall, a government official in Washington wrote an internal memo warning that planes would continue to fall from the sky. They would crash into homes, businesses, and city streets, "in many cases resulting in damage to property and life," and there was little that authorities could do to prevent that from happening.

But these authorities could stop the women—and they would. Henderson would see to it himself. The man who took credit for inviting the women to fly in the Powder Puff Derby, and who had personally invited Klingensmith to participate in Chicago, now said he was opposed to women racing airplanes. "Miss Florence Klingensmith's fatal crash in Chicago in 1933, in a closed-course race, only proved what I already knew," he declared.

Women didn't belong in his races.

They were out.

CHAPTER 26
ALL THINGS BEING EQUAL

*L*ouise Thaden didn't make it to Fargo that September for Klingensmith's funeral. She was living in Kansas City at the time with her husband and two-year-old son—and nine months pregnant with her second child. The baby—a daughter—was due to be born any day now. But getting the news of Klingensmith's death, and how the men had treated her, would have been crushing to Thaden. Every day, she thought about flying.

In the months before she got pregnant, Thaden tried to set a new female endurance record, flying nonstop over Long Island for a week or longer—twenty-four hours a day. She would refuel in the sky with a hose dropped from another airplane. For the job, Thaden would need a copilot. Organizers paired her up with Frances Marsalis, a likable and experienced pilot from Texas. And together, not long after Earhart's ocean flight, the two women took off over New York in a small cabin plane.

It was not a glamorous adventure. By night, Thaden and Marsalis froze in the cold, huddled beneath a thin wool blanket. By day, they struggled to stay awake, making circle after circle around the airfield, about two thousand feet off the ground.

In the end, Thaden and Marsalis broke the female endurance record after five days—and kept flying. But after 196 consecutive hours in the sky—more than eight days—they decided they'd had enough.

"It's over, gal," Thaden said, reaching over and rumpling Marsalis's dark hair on the morning of the last day. "We're going to land."

On the ground that night, the women celebrated. But the party didn't last long. Thaden was soon back home, raising her son, getting pregnant with her daughter, and trying to juggle her career—flying—with her love for her kids. It wasn't easy. While Nichols and Earhart were pushing each other across oceans, and while Klingensmith was challenging the men, Thaden was sitting in the sandbox with her young son and wondering if her days of competitive flying were over. She was

Thaden, sitting here with her son, Bill, and the family dog, felt the pressures of many modern working mothers: she wanted to fly, but had responsibilities at home. *Thaden Family Collection*

twenty-seven years old—and feeling torn. "Torn between two loves," she wrote. Her flying and her family, her career and her children.

Her baby girl was born in Kansas City less than three weeks after Klingensmith's death in Chicago. And the proud parents, Herb and Louise, announced the exciting news to their friends in a letter. The girl's name was Patricia, they said. "Pat to you!"

Thaden had a family of four, two healthy children, a boy and a girl—a good life. Still, she was restless, itching to fly again—even now, after Klingensmith's death.

====

The female pilots of the Ninety-Nines honored Klingensmith that month. She wasn't just an original Ninety-Nine, they said; she was important—a pilot "who died proving that women can fly on an equal basis with men." That kind of bravery deserved a heroic place in American history. "More particularly," the Ninety-Nines said, "in the history of **feminism**." And yet, here was Henderson using Klingensmith's death as an excuse to ban the women from the air races. It was the worst kind of insult. Especially because, in late 1933, the women had enough problems as it was.

They struggled to get aviation jobs—almost any job at all. The Ninety-Nines believed men didn't want them at the airfield or around the hangar, and the organization finally set out to prove it was true. They mailed surveys late that year to almost every plane manufacturer, supplier, and airline in the country requesting information about the women they employed, the types of jobs they held, and their worth to the company compared to men. Question: "What jobs if any do you feel that women are better fitted for than men?" Question: "Would you keep a woman in a job that you feel a man could do equally well?" Question: "Why do you not use women in larger numbers?"

The companies that returned the surveys didn't hold back. Women, they said, were best suited for office jobs—answering the phone or typing letters—or serving "as hostesses" on board planes flown by men. As a result, the companies saw little need to hire many women, excluding them for lots of reasons. "Limited positions . . . Our business calls for more men . . . All things being equal, prefer men."

———

"I want to warn you," Nichols told anyone who asked, "that opportunities for work, for women in aviation, have become almost impossible."

The situation had been bad before the Depression; it was worse now. The surveys confirmed it, and Klingensmith's death only complicated matters. The men had already been blocking women from aviation jobs. Now they could argue that women didn't belong in a cockpit—period. Didn't belong in the races. Didn't deserve a stake of the prize money. Ruth Nichols knew what that felt like. She knew what it was like to be excluded, left out. She was among the many women struggling that year.

Crosley wasn't interested in backing her anymore. And it wasn't the only source of income drying up for her. Just a few years earlier, Nichols had charged as much as five hundred dollars to give a speech. Now she was lucky to get fifty dollars for an appearance or even to be invited at all. Still, Nichols was dreaming, planning something big. "A long over-water record next summer," she said. She couldn't be the first woman to fly across the ocean— Earhart had beaten her to it. But maybe Nichols could be the first female pilot to go around the world. "This is," she said, "the last important news flight left."

But corporations weren't interested in helping her. One by one, they passed on Nichols's around-the-world flight, making it clear that Ruth Nichols, like the other women, was going nowhere. By 1934, there was maybe only one woman with enough power to convince moneyed men, race organizers, and Henderson to listen.

CHAPTER 27
MEN PILOTS ONLY

*A*melia Earhart stepped into a church, packed full of people, ready to deliver her talk. The large Tuesday-night crowd—about fifteen hundred people in all—was unusual for Mason City, Iowa; on this night, in the fall of 1933, it felt like half the town was there. But to Earhart, it was just another night. As soon as she was finished in Mason City, she was heading to Minneapolis and Des Moines, where she was getting three hundred dollars to appear.

Her talk—"Flying for Fun"—was almost always the same. But Earhart made her audience feel as if she had crafted the words just for them. She wanted people to know that flying was safe and getting safer; that one day soon everyone would travel by plane. "It is coming much faster than we realize," Earhart said. She made it clear that, yes, flying was more dangerous than traveling by horse and buggy or oxcart. "But," Earhart liked to add, "I didn't see any oxcarts around this building this evening."

In her speeches that fall, she didn't talk about Klingensmith's death or the growing fight with the men at the air races. But anyone who attended her talks understood how Earhart felt. For years now, the former social worker had been pointing out the ways that men mistreated the female pilots—especially after a crash. "When a man cracks up, no one pays any special attention," Earhart said. "But oh, when a girl does . . ." Here came the questions and the criticism, fair or not.

It bothered Earhart, who had long ago developed a keen sense of justice. "Women," she said during one stop at Yale University that November, "should be treated no differently from men." Earhart even argued that women should serve as soldiers. "They should be drafted," she said, "made to do the dirty work, and real fighting." If nothing else, Earhart said, it would discourage old male politicians from pushing the country into battle. "They are the ones," she said, "who start war."

—

Cliff Henderson was at the center of the war between the male and female pilots.

As the air races resumed in 1934, Henderson wasn't backing away from the idea that women shouldn't race. At the first national air meet after Klingensmith's death, scheduled to take place in New Orleans during Mardi Gras in February 1934, race organizers banned women. The reason, Henderson told reporters, was simple.

"Obviously," he said, "the unfortunate death of Florence Klingensmith contributed to this decision." But really, for Henderson, the decision just made sense. "There is no more place for women pilots in the high-speed, free-for-all air race game," he said, "than there is a place for women drivers on the speedway at Indianapolis." Or, he added, on a football field.

Local leaders in New Orleans didn't object to Henderson's ban, welcoming the air-race promoter to the city in late 1933. He spoke at downtown luncheons, promising thrills from some of the top male fliers in America.

Zantford Granville, the builder of the speedy Gee Bee, would be there. Captain Merle Nelson, an airman famous for performing "night-fire rides," spitting fireworks from his plane while flying three hundred miles an hour in the dark, was coming too. Lee Miles, a record-holding pilot, would be racing every day, Henderson promised, as would two other famous aviators: Roscoe Turner, a Los Angeles pilot built like a linebacker, and Benny Howard, a Chicago airman tall and thin as a pencil. Together, Turner and Howard had more speed records, race wins, and trophies than almost any other two pilots combined. Better still, they were colorful characters. Turner even flew with a pet lion named Gilmore.

———

With airmen like these, Henderson didn't need women in his races in 1934. And a large crowd turned out for opening day in New Orleans, proving him right.

But the race fans had hardly settled into their seats before things began going wrong. Rounding a pylon on a test flight that afternoon, a pilot crashed. He survived—a miracle. But the races almost didn't. For the next four days, heavy rains made flying

While the women protested, Benny Howard, left, and Roscoe Turner, right, kept flying, establishing themselves as two of the fastest pilots in America. Unbeatable, many believed. *Smithsonian National Air and Space Museum (NASM A-5194-B)*

impossible, forcing Henderson to do something he'd never done: cancel. The Mardi Gras races would have to begin on Ash Wednesday, he announced, promising to honor any tickets purchased in advance.

But people coming to the races that Wednesday didn't get a chance to see Zantford Granville. On his way to New Orleans, he crashed in South Carolina in his blue-and-yellow Gee Bee for reasons unknown. He was flying roughly as high as Klingensmith had been at the time of her crash, about seventy feet off the ground. But no one questioned whether Granville should have bailed out, recovered, or saved himself. He surely did everything he could before crashing, nose-first, into the ground, and getting killed, with a list of injuries almost exactly like Klingensmith's.

Granville's family buried him that week in Massachusetts while Henderson's all-male races finally got off the ground. The skies were clear after days of bad weather, and Henderson had an exciting show planned for the fans. That night, Captain Merle

Nelson took to the sky for his night-fire ride, spitting a stream of fireworks from his plane in the dark.

The show didn't last long. At 8:52 p.m., twenty minutes after taking off, Nelson crashed in full view of the crowd. The aircraft burst into flames on impact and skidded across the ground like a rolling fireball. It was a terrible crash that killed Nelson and stunned Henderson.

"This is one of the greatest surprises of my life," he said. "If we feared for any of the fliers, we feared least of all for Captain Nelson's safety."

It was, for Henderson, just the beginning of his problems. That Saturday, just three days after Nelson's crash, a parachute jumper got hung up on the tail of a plane two thousand feet above the grandstand. In his effort to shake off the tangled parachute and save the jumper, the pilot lost control and plunged both of them into a large lake north of New Orleans.

Boaters hurried to the crash site to find the parachute jumper still tangled up on the tail—and dead. The pilot died too. It would be almost a month before his body washed ashore. And by then, Cliff Henderson was long gone, returned to Cleveland.

Henderson was already planning the next air races, set to take place over Labor Day weekend in Cleveland. Once again, the women were not invited to compete because, of course, according to him, they didn't know how to fly.

CHAPTER 28
THAT'S WHAT I THINK OF WIVES FLYING

*I*n the races that Henderson was planning to put on in Cleveland in September 1934, the women would be allowed to do only one thing: parachute-jump. No flying. For the second air meet in a row, they were out—a rule that the women would not accept. In late July, one month before the Cleveland races were to begin, the new president of the Ninety-Nines, Margaret Cooper, demanded that the women be included. "The '99' girls are up in arms," Cooper said. "We feel it is only fair to recognize our presence as contestants."

Henderson fired back at Cooper, claiming that he had always supported the women. "If any individual has championed women's participation in competitive aviation during the past six years," he told Cooper, "it has been myself. And I have done so in the face of protest and ridicule of all types." But that was over now.

"I shall never forgive myself," he told the women, "for not reacting to my personal 'hunches' in protesting against permitting Florence Klingensmith to enter the mixed competition in Chicago last

Labor Day." Others had approved Klingensmith's participation, of course, including the contest committee, the officials on the field that day, the emcee, and, by extension, Henderson himself. But it had all been a mistake, Henderson said now.

The women, upset over Henderson's rules, quickly made a decision. Earhart, Thaden, Nichols, and others were boycotting the 1934 Cleveland races. If they couldn't compete against the men, the women would hold their own air meet—the first-ever women's national air meet that August in Dayton, Ohio.

The crowds there were expected to be much smaller than usual—a few thousand race fans per day, at most. The prizes would be smaller too. Even the racecourse itself seemed small. In place of fifty-foot steel pylons, the women in Dayton would fly their planes around other items: a truck in a farmer's field, a barn in a nearby town, thirty-five-foot poles, and a local landmark, the Waco Aircraft factory, where an executive had recently encouraged women to stay in the kitchen "making homes pleasant."

Only about a dozen pilots showed up to compete, less famous women, mostly, or those in need of money. Frances Marsalis, Thaden's copilot in the 1932 endurance record, was one of them. She was focused on the big-money race of the weekend, Sunday's fifty-mile free-for-all around a triangular course. The winner would take home one thousand dollars. "And boy, how I need that $1,000," Marsalis told others in Dayton.

In the race that Sunday, Marsalis came from behind, picking off her competitors one by one. By the fifth and final lap, she was only sixty seconds off the lead and closing in on the leaders at pylon no. 2, in a potato field. Several planes were soon bunched up together, each of them banking hard and low. But Marsalis pushed her plane even lower than the others, skimming across the ground—too low. The left wing on Marsalis's plane hit the ground, driving her down into a cloud of dust.

The plane began to roll, tumbling across the field a dozen times before finally skidding to a halt. While Marsalis's competitors raced for the finish line, judges and farmers ran across the potato field, hoping to save the woman inside the airplane. They called for an ambulance, but it was too late. Marsalis was dead.

Thaden read the news in her morning paper, stunned. Another Ninety-Nine down. Thaden and Nichols comforted themselves with the idea that Marsalis would have wanted to go this way. "When my time comes," Marsalis said once, "I hope it's in a plane where I can crack up in one grand splurge." But the women also knew that Marsalis's death would hurt them all. Henderson, in Cleveland, was already using it against them. He had told the women they couldn't race. They hadn't listened—and now another one of them was dead.

"Everyone knows that it's not that I have anything against women fliers because they are women," Henderson said after Marsalis's crash, appearing nervous, for once, before reporters in

Cleveland. He claimed just to be speaking the truth, doing what was best for aviation. "And Frances Marsalis's death has again proved my theory is right."

———

The daily newspapers in Cleveland supported Henderson. The *Plain Dealer,* the *News,* and the *Press* all published stories suggesting Henderson was right to exclude the women. They quoted pilots saying as much. "Flying is a man's business," one male aviator said. And to prove they were being fair to the female pilots, the newspapers also quoted women on the subject—women who agreed with Henderson.

"I do not believe women, as a rule, are equipped for racing," said Gertrude Chester, a licensed pilot and wife of a pilot from Illinois who had come to Cleveland for the races. "My husband wouldn't think of me entering an event against him, and doesn't think I should do any racing at all. And I quite agree." She believed women belonged on the ground at the races, and others believed women belonged on the ground at all times. "Imagine a jockey's wife being a jockey just because her husband is one," one female critic said in Cleveland. "Or a truck driver's wife riding around with him on his deliveries." It was ridiculous, the woman argued. Silly, even. "That's what I think of wives flying."

The races kicked off that Friday in Cleveland with thirty-eight thousand fans gathered to cheer on the Bendix Trophy racers. Fans had been hoping to greet Roscoe Turner and Benny Howard. But mechanical failures and mishaps knocked them out of the race before it even began. So people had to settle for Doug Davis, a decorated flier, airline pilot, husband, and father of two young children. It was Davis who showed up first in the Bendix, winning forty-five hundred dollars. And it was Davis returning to the sky that Monday in the twelve-lap, hundred-mile Thompson Trophy free-for-all. Like Klingensmith and Marsalis, he was going to race around pylons placed on the ground.

The race worried Davis. Roscoe Turner was going to be there for this one; his plane had been repaired. Benny Howard would make it too. He wasn't flying, but he was going to send his most trusted pilot up in one of his Howard race planes. "I've half a notion not to enter at all," Davis admitted that Saturday. "Someone's going to get killed." But the winner was going to take home another forty-five hundred dollars, and Davis wanted that cash. "Bring home some money this time, Dad," his six-year-old son had told him before he left Georgia for the races. "We've got enough trophies."

One of the largest crowds in air-race history turned out for the event that Monday, an estimated quarter of a million fans. Everyone was waiting to see the big event, and they watched as Doug Davis quickly shot to the front of the pack. By the fifth lap, it was a two-man race: Davis and Turner—no other plane was even close—with Davis leading by just a few hundred feet. Then, on the eighth lap, Davis made a mistake. He cut the corner, darting inside the pylon. Knowing he had to circle back and go around it to avoid disqualification, he banked his plane hard, shot five hundred feet into the sky, and prepared to turn, dive, and pass outside the pylon this time. But he never made it. In the turn, Davis's plane began to tumble, spiraling toward the ground.

"He's going to crash," the race announcer said with a gasp. "His plane shot straight up in the air and then disappeared behind the trees."

With Davis crashing and the other planes lagging behind, Turner cruised to victory. The race was over and the crowd was now focused on Davis and his crash, four miles to the west. At first, they were convinced he must have survived. The man knew what he was doing, after all. Henderson believed Davis's injuries had to be minor and finally agreed to have this amazing news announced to the crowd.

But Turner, who had seen Davis go down, pressed for more details.

"Are you sure?" Turner kept asking at the finish line. "Are you sure that Doug is all right? I didn't see him get out."

No one had seen a parachute on the horizon. And no one was watching Davis strolling across the field. They hadn't seen it because Davis hadn't made it. A crowd of thirty-five hundred people—people "mad with excitement," one police officer said— were the first ones to make the discovery. Running across the field, they arrived at the wreckage before race officials could, and then fought one another at the scene. They weren't looking to rescue the pilot. They just wanted souvenirs from his remains, his clothes, and his red-and-black airplane, claiming anything they could carry away. Davis was dead, killed on impact.

To honor Davis the next night, the air races booked a thirty-minute radio show. And Henderson personally attended his funeral. The crash wasn't Davis's fault. A chunk of wing, four feet wide and eighteen inches long, had ripped away under the strain of the speed, sending Davis to his death. "It's a wonder there aren't more racing pilots killed," one official said afterward.

CHAPTER 29

AN EXCELLENT TYPE OF WOMAN

A melia Earhart looked out on the crowd of women at the Waldorf Astoria hotel in New York City. It was late September, three weeks after Doug Davis's death in Cleveland, and Earhart wished she had a better report to give the crowd interested in hearing her thoughts about women's place in the sky. "Two capital Ts stand in the way of their progress," she told the women in the room. "One is Training—or lack of it. The other, Tradition."

Earhart had recently celebrated her thirty-seventh birthday and, if anything, was becoming more radical with time, refusing to believe in the notion of a "woman's place." "Her place," Earhart said, "is wherever her individual aptitude places her." Or it should be, anyway. "And the work of married men and women should be split," Earhart added. "She should taste the grind of earning a living—and he should learn the stupidity of housework."

Six blocks away that afternoon, a small army of dedicated women were at work inside the office of the Ninety-Nines. They were taking on Cliff Henderson, his races, and his rules. The women weren't just writing letters pleading with Henderson. They called him out publicly late that summer, in a two-page article titled "Cliff Henderson Turns Back the Clock."

In the article, the women pointed out they had been racing since 1929, and if they'd been good enough to be included then, they were certainly good enough now, no matter what had happened to Florence Klingensmith or Frances Marsalis. Men died in the races all the time, the article pointed out, yet no one talked about canceling because of their deaths. No one talked about banning the men. "Women are invited to cooperate," the Ninety-Nines wrote, "by sitting in the grandstand." But they wanted the same shot at living or dying in the sky. As Ruth Nichols said, "Women have the same right to be killed in airplane races as men have."

The women, meeting late that summer, even voted on it.

"Be it resolved," they declared, "that we protest the discrimination against women fliers, eliminating them from the schedule of events of the 1934 National Air Races. . . .

"Be it resolved," they said, "that we protest the name 'National Air Races' being applied to any event in which women do not have fair representation."

And "be it resolved" that they would oppose any future efforts to keep them out of the races because "such action is prejudiced, unjust, and without any foundation whatsoever."

Even the reporters—almost all men—could no longer defend Henderson. He had banned the women after Klingensmith's death.

But Davis had died in almost exactly the same way, proving that air racing could kill anyone—male or female. In September 1934, aviation editors from America's biggest newspapers voted to support including women in the races.

Then, in January 1935, Earhart set out to make another daring and historic flight—a flight that would prove women could do anything.

As usual, it began in secret.

Just after Christmas, Earhart arrived by luxury ocean liner in Hawaii with her husband, Putnam, a Hollywood pilot named Paul Mantz, and her red Lockheed. While she went sightseeing, Mantz tested the new radio on her plane. If everything worked as Mantz hoped, Earhart would be able to speak to America from the middle of the ocean.

He soon reported the good news to Putnam: the radio was working. It was time for Earhart to leave Hawaii for California, alone again in an airplane. The world's transatlantic heroine now hoped to be the first woman to fly solo across the Pacific.

The flight was roughly twenty-four hundred miles—and for the first time, really, Earhart was facing criticism for her plans. "The American public is devoted to Amelia Earhart because she is an excellent type of woman, sensible and wholesome," one Hawaiian reporter wrote, but this time she had gone too far. As one critic pointed out, "There is nothing to be gained by flying solo from Hawaii to the mainland in a single-engined land plane."

The criticism hurt Earhart. Still, she was going. On a Friday afternoon two weeks after she had arrived in Hawaii, Earhart and Putnam drove to the muddy airfield where Mantz had been preparing her plane. Then, hardly saying goodbye, she climbed up a ladder and settled into the cockpit of her plane. The engine was running; everything was ready. Everything but Earhart herself.

"Not yet," she told the ground crew.

A minute later, she waved to the men outside, taxied the plane to the runway, gunned the engine, and took off. She was up and away just before 5:00 p.m., flying to the tip of the island, then banking northeast toward the open ocean and the long, moonless night ahead of her—a night filled with all the usual dangers. Storms, clouds, fog, and the unknown.

The radio didn't work at first; there was nothing but static.

"Speak louder," Putnam begged Earhart from the ground more than two hours into the flight. They couldn't hear her. But soon the messages were coming in. And it wasn't just Putnam who heard her. Ordinary Americans listened too, hearing Earhart's voice on their radios inside their living rooms.

9:47 p.m.: "All is well."

12:45 a.m.: "Everything okay."

3:45 a.m.: "I am becoming quite tired."

Finally, dawn broke over the ocean—she was close to her goal. Or she hoped she was. Honestly, Earhart wasn't totally sure where she was as she flew over blankets of fog. "I should be near, if the course is correct," she said. "Heading for Oakland."

By 1935, crowds surged around Earhart wherever she went, including this landing in Oakland. *Courtesy of Purdue University Libraries, Karnes Archives and Special Collections*

On the ground, at the airport where Thaden had once gotten her start, ten thousand people had been waiting for hours. When Earhart's red plane finally appeared in the sky, they could wait no longer. The crowd pushed past police and swarmed around Earhart. A truck even had to cut a path through the crowd just to get her into a hangar. Here, tired and covered in grime, she leaned against a wall, resting but not for long. Five months later she would make another record flight: flying nonstop from Mexico City to New Jersey.

Surely she could compete against men in the air races.

CHAPTER 30
THEY'LL BE IN OUR HAIR

*I*t was strangely cold in late August 1935 when the men and the women arrived in Cleveland for the races. In private conversations, away from the field, Roscoe Turner supported the female pilots. "It is my belief that a man or woman, provided they have no serious handicap, can do almost anything they make up their minds to do," he said once, "if they keep trying." But Turner made no such comments to the press, choosing instead to keep his silence.

Benny Howard stayed quiet too. He taught his wife, Maxine, how to fly, and fly fast. Yet racing was out of the question. "I wouldn't let her," Howard said. He seemed to prefer that she wait for him on the ground and greet him with a kiss.

In a men-only pilots' meeting in Cleveland, other airmen agreed. They voted to maintain Henderson's ban, preferring that the women held their own races somewhere else. But Howard's star pilot, Harold Neumann, pointed out a flaw with the men's plans.

"I'm afraid there will be trouble," he said, "unless the women have at least one race."

Henderson, under pressure, agreed. He offered the women three races in 1935, including a chance to compete in the Bendix Trophy race, if they wanted it. Forget about everything he had said in the past or how he had treated the women in 1934; 1935, he said, was going to be different. "The women will be in the foreground of the picture."

That was one way of putting it. Veteran racer Lee Miles put it another way. The women, Miles said after the pilots' meeting in Cleveland, were about to ruin the picture. "The first thing you know they'll want to borrow our planes," Miles complained. He spoke for most of his fellow airmen when he announced that he wished the women were out of the air races for good. "If we let them in," Miles said, "they'll be in our hair and become pests."

———

Cliff Henderson was all smiles as the races began in Cleveland that summer. He had ended the fight with the women and he was already using them to advertise the races—"the world's most spectacular presentation," he was calling it.

Thaden was listed among those expected to attend. But it wasn't true. As the air races opened, Thaden was home, far from Cleveland, and looking for a job. She and Herb were struggling; not broke, exactly, but close. Her best hope was getting hired at the U.S. Department of Commerce as an air-marking pilot. In 1935, aviators could still easily get lost, especially in bad weather, and they crashed and sometimes died as a result. Air-marking pilots helped to prevent that by identifying barns or factories with large roofs on which the government could paint the names of nearby towns. It was almost the only job a female aviator could get in 1935—and Thaden needed it. Finally, she got hired. As Henderson's races opened in Cleveland, the government agreed to pay her $2,600 per year.

Thaden wasn't going to Cleveland; she likely couldn't afford it. Nichols wasn't going either. In August 1935, she felt lucky to have a regular job too. A friend had purchased three large passenger planes, called Curtiss Condors, to start a new East Coast airline and asked Nichols to be a copilot. "And he didn't have to ask twice," Nichols said. "I would have taken the job for nothing." For the first time in almost two years, she was flying again. Nichols assisted a male pilot at the controls of a large Condor on a tour across the Northeast, giving joy rides, essentially, to help advertise the new airline. It wasn't racing or setting records, but it was flying, and that was better than nothing.

Only Earhart could take Henderson up on his challenge in 1935.

—

The purse for the Bendix that August was ten thousand dollars—four times Thaden's new annual salary—and it drew the usual group of hopefuls. On the day of the race, nine aviators gathered at the starting line at a small airport in Burbank near Los Angeles. The fastest time to Cleveland would win.

Roscoe Turner was there, boasting that his gold plane could

hit speeds more than three hundred miles an hour. But to finish first, he was going to have to beat Benny Howard, who was also expecting victory in a new white plane he was calling *Mister Mulligan*. Competitors figured *Mister Mulligan* would max out at around a hundred and eighty miles an hour—not fast enough to beat Turner or Cecil Allen, another man competing in the Bendix. Allen—a square-jawed adventurer—was flying a red Gee Bee, one of Granville's dangerous planes. And there, among the men, stood two women, each looking to make history. Earhart was preparing to fly to Cleveland in her now famous red Lockheed, while another woman, Jacqueline Cochran, was vowing to get to Cleveland without a single stop.

Cochran barely even made it off the ground in Burbank. She nearly crashed her plane on takeoff and then quit just three hundred miles in. She'd been forced down in Arizona by radio problems and chose to stay there—finished. If a woman was going to win the Bendix, it would have to be Earhart. And she got away first, taking off just before 1:00 a.m. and banking hard for Cleveland, 2,046 miles away. It was a perfect takeoff, cheered by five thousand people in the dark. But Earhart quickly fell off the pace. By the time she reached New Mexico at 5:25 that morning, Earhart was two hours behind Turner, already out of contention for the Bendix Trophy, and she knew it.

But at least she was still flying, pushing on to Cleveland, no matter her time. Two of her male competitors had been forced down with engine problems; they were out. And Allen, with his

Gee Bee, crashed on takeoff in California. The Gee Bee went down just three miles from the runway, plowing into a field while residents of North Hollywood watched in horror. They could see the red plane was out of control, wobbling, falling, then cartwheeling across the ground. "A vicious cartwheel," one witness said, "that tore it to pieces." Cecil Allen was dead.

Unaware of Allen's death, Howard and Turner flew on, streaking toward Cleveland in some of the worst weather they had ever experienced. Rain and wind and storms.

Howard went high to dodge the worst of the conditions, flying along at twenty thousand feet, while Turner did the opposite, flying close to the ground. The two men had no way of knowing it—separated as they were in the sky. But they were tied, wing tip to wing tip, in a dead heat for the Bendix Trophy and the prize money.

On the ground in Cleveland, heavy rains kept the crowds away. There were just a couple of thousand people in the stands when the first racer appeared in the sky.

It was Howard.

"Where's that man, Roscoe?" Howard asked as soon as he climbed out of *Mister Mulligan*.

Howard had arrived in Cleveland first, coming in at 1:40 p.m. But Turner had left Los Angeles one hour and forty-three minutes after his rival, meaning he had until 3:23 p.m. to get there and beat Howard, forcing everyone to sit—and wait.

Two o'clock came and went. And there was no Turner.

Three o'clock came. No Turner.

Reporters began to tell Howard that he could start celebrating. But he refused to accept victory. "Wait," he said, "until Turner gets here."

Finally, at exactly 3:23 p.m., the last possible moment, Turner came in low from the west, sending officials scrambling for the official timer. They needed to make sure they had their calculations right before announcing the winner. They ran the math and made their announcement.

Howard had won the Bendix by twenty-three and a half seconds.

"The closest shave I've had," he said, "in ten years of flying."

It was just the beginning of a big weekend for Howard. He swept the races, winning again and again, and proving that *Mister Mulligan* was the fastest plane not only over long distances but also in short bursts.

Earhart, on the other hand, finished last in the Bendix, fifth place—more than five hours slower than Howard's white airplane. If women were ever going to win in races like this, they would need better planes and better luck.

They would need a miracle.

CHAPTER 31
ON THE SIDELINES

*B*ack in Wichita, Kansas, plane manufacturer Walter Beech was watching, waiting—and building a fast airplane of his own. He had sold his original company, Travel Air, years earlier. He had briefly worked for others and had even moved away from Wichita in the early years of the Great Depression. But by 1935, he was back in Kansas with a new plan and a young wife. Beech had fallen for his secretary, Olive Ann Mellor.

Her job, in the beginning for Beech, was to answer the phones and help get people excited about Beech's planes by selling rides in them for a dollar apiece. But Mellor was good with numbers, good at math. She had been paying the family bills since she was eleven years old. And over time, things changed—both in the workplace and between Beech and Mellor. In 1930, the couple got married, and the secretary was soon known as O. A. Beech, a powerful and mysterious woman. She could be both friendly and tough. The sort of woman who would never forget a person's birthday but could also fire someone on the spot. As one friend later put it, "Nobody knows Olive Ann Beech."

Back in Wichita, the husband-and-wife team launched their new aircraft company. They were calling it Beechcraft, and they were sure it would succeed. The key, Walter thought, was building planes that were safer—but also faster. The first Beechcraft—the Model 17—was eye-catching, anyway. The wings on the new biplane were staggered—with the top wing positioned almost two feet behind the lower. It was also sleek and modern, with seats for five and a 420-horsepower engine in the nose. But sales were slow. Walter and Olive Ann needed a breakthrough.

Walter hit the road selling Beechcraft—the name, his company—until, finally, orders began to come in. In 1934, the company built eighteen planes. The next year, it produced twice that number, and the Beeches had reason to be hopeful about 1936

too. Their newest Staggerwing—the C17R—had enough speed to compete in air races. Maybe even the biggest race of them all.

Olive Ann wanted to win the Bendix, pitting their Wichita airship against Roscoe Turner's golden plane and Benny

Olive Ann Beech started as Walter Beech's secretary in Wichita, Kan., but was soon instrumental in running his start-up airplane company, Beechcraft. *Courtesy of Mary Lynn Beech Oliver*

Howard's unbeatable *Mister Mulligan*. She just needed someone to fly it, and Olive Ann had an idea for that, too.

Perhaps they should choose a woman, she said.

———

Ruth Nichols was the kind of woman who deserved the job: a veteran pilot who was both famous and calm in the cockpit. In late 1935, while working for that new airline on the East Coast, Nichols was cool, even after it became clear that the giant plane she was copiloting was going down in New York.

The promotional trip across the Northeast had, until that moment, been exactly like all the others in recent weeks—smooth and easy. But on this morning, the problems began just after takeoff. The plane's left engine died with a boom as soon as it climbed into the air, and the large plane immediately began to lose altitude.

Nichols and the pilot, Harry Hublitz, didn't panic. They remained in their seats, fighting for control of the plane as it dove into a grove of trees. On impact, the cockpit cracked open like an egg, and the plane burst into flames. Hublitz—seriously injured but still conscious—crawled to safety through a hole in the cockpit. The crew in back, mostly unharmed, did the same, and then one of them returned to save Nichols by dragging her away from the fire.

She was a mess, with broken bones in her arms, legs, and face and serious burns on her skin. Newspapers across the country reported that Nichols might not make it. But it was Hublitz who died from his injuries that night. Nichols, the ultimate survivor, had dodged death again.

"Dear Rufus," Earhart wrote her from a lecture stop in Michigan not long after her crash. "I am so sorry. Do get well as soon as possible as we women pilots can't afford to have you sitting on the sidelines for long."

But Nichols was almost thirty-five years old, and she could feel it.

She was finished. For all the miles she had traveled, for all the places she had gone, she was soon right back where she had started: at her parents' home in Rye, recovering from her injuries and not flying anytime soon.

CHAPTER 32
THE CHANCE OF A LIFETIME

*T*hat December, while Nichols returned home, Earhart was laid up in New York as well, suffering from a bad cold. Earhart's illness, at least, was temporary. By the middle of the month, she was back on the road, giving one of the 136 lectures that Putnam had scheduled for her that winter. She needed to be out there talking and preparing for the new year, 1936.

Olive Ann Beech had always admired Earhart. But Earhart didn't need the Beeches' new fast airplane in Wichita. Putnam was working to get his wife an airship that was all hers, one that was powerful enough to set transcontinental speed records and reliable enough for a secret flight—a trip around the world.

At first, Earhart and Putnam spoke about these plans to no one. Earhart claimed to be taking a break. "Right now," she said, "I've stopped being a personality in order to be a person." She did the talks that Putnam had scheduled for her. But she was also settling into an unlikely job in an unlikely place. The president of Purdue University, a college in rural Indiana, had hired Earhart. He offered her two thousand dollars for just a few weeks of work on campus.

Earhart was thrilled to be at Purdue, impressing the young female college students from the start with her first, and possibly only, rule: No one was allowed to call her Mrs. Putnam. "Even my own husband," she told the students, "would call me Miss Earhart." She ate with them in the dining hall, walked with them to class, and encouraged them to ask her questions while she asked them some questions of her own. "Are you planning to seek employment after you leave college? . . . Do you plan to continue working after marriage?" And this one: "What do you think a married man's part in running the household should be?"

When Earhart left campus at the end of November, she announced the findings of her survey. Ninety-two percent of female students at Purdue told Earhart they planned to work after college, and almost half the freshman women already knew what they wanted to do. Earhart was excited about her findings and shared them with the newspapers. But she was probably not as excited as Putnam. He had convinced Purdue officials to help buy a new Lockheed Electra plane for Earhart.

The Purdue Research Foundation would put up forty thousand dollars to help buy a new Lockheed, a modern airship Earhart called her Flying Laboratory. She was trying to suggest that the plane would be used to further scientific knowledge. But privately, Putnam was more honest, promising Purdue that his wife would fly the plane to pursue records—important flights.

Starting with the Bendix race.

She collected the plane in July 1936 and began to prepare.

<hr style="width:10%"/>

Thaden and Earhart had been drifting apart. It wasn't just that Thaden didn't like Earhart's husband; it was that, increasingly, she didn't understand Earhart. While Thaden was trying to be a wife, a mother, and an aviator—a balancing act that didn't always work—Earhart seemed to be pushing herself to the point of recklessness. Thaden thought Earhart's solo flight from Hawaii to California had been too risky, and she told Earhart as much.

"Would you mind telling me sometime in strict confidence why the heck you DO things like that? I'd really like to know," Thaden told Earhart.

Thaden considered Earhart one of her best friends—one of her only friends—and yet, also, a mystery. "When it comes down to brass tacks, I don't know you at all," Thaden told Earhart. "I doubt anyone does."

Thaden, by comparison, didn't feel mysterious at all. She felt almost ordinary, actually—a terrible feeling. In order to make ends meet, she had returned home to Arkansas and moved in with her parents. Herb's time in Kansas City had come to an end. In his new job, he was traveling too much. Then Louise had gone and gotten hired as an air-marking pilot, meaning she, too, would be traveling now, flying across the country to paint city names on the roofs of barns and warehouses.

The job was important to her. She wanted to make aviation

safer—and not just because of Nichols's crash in New York. That winter, while Thaden was on an air-marking trip out West, a plane went down in a snowstorm, killing two men on board. The crash would have gone unnoticed by Thaden had it not been for the man at the controls: Dewey Noyes. He was the husband of an old friend—Blanche Noyes, the fourth-place finisher in the 1929 Powder Puff Derby and one of the original Ninety-Nines.

Without him, Noyes was lost, crying all the time. "She is pretty well shot to pieces," Earhart said. So she did what a friend would do. Earhart pushed to get Noyes hired as an air-marker, working with Thaden.

Noyes joined Thaden that summer, and Thaden was happy to see her. Thaden was far from home, away from her husband and children, and also grieving that summer. Her father, Roy—a traveling salesman—had died that June in a car crash north of Bentonville.

Blanche Noyes, left, Thaden, second from left, and two other female aviators were lucky to get hired as "air-markers," making flying safer. *Thaden Family Collection*

It had been a hard year. But instead of disappearing into sadness, Thaden grew bold. In July, she went to the air races in Denver. Ten days later, for the first time in years, she climbed back into a plane to set a new

In July 1936, Walter and Olive Ann Beech took their newest Beechcraft to Denver to compete in the regional air races there. A month later, Olive Ann decided to enter it in the Bendix. *Courtesy of Mary Lynn Beech Oliver*

female record. She flew a pylon course in Virginia at an average speed of 109 miles an hour—surprising speed for a lightweight plane. Then, late one night that summer, back on the air-marking trail with Noyes, Thaden got a phone call from Olive Ann Beech. Olive Ann was offering her the chance of a lifetime—a spot in the ten-thousand-dollar Bendix race, with an additional twenty-five hundred dollars to be awarded to the first woman to finish.

"I think we might as well have that money," Olive Ann said, "don't you?"

CHAPTER 33
WE ARE GOING TO FLY

*T*haden almost said no.

At first, she thought about turning down Olive Ann's offer to fly in the Bendix. The race was too dangerous. In five years of Bendix races, almost half of the thirty-five pilots who had competed had failed to finish, and ten of them had gone down, due to unpredictable problems. Fires, empty gas tanks, broken fuel lines, busted radios, and, of course, crashes. But in the end, she accepted Olive Ann's offer—and her challenge—asking her coworker, Blanche Noyes, to join her.

For the reporters, it was a cute story. A year earlier, race officials had allowed Earhart and another woman to fly in the Bendix, but only if a man flew with them. The idea that two women might fly together was almost a joke. Some even suggested that this year's Bendix should be organized into two divisions: one for the men, who were trying to win it all, and one for the women, who were clearly just trying to claim the twenty-five-hundred-dollar consolation prize set aside for the fastest female.

They weren't going to win, these women. Not Thaden and Noyes in their Beechcraft. Not Earhart, joined in her new Flying Laboratory by female copilot Helen Richey. And not Laura Ingalls, either. Ingalls, the third female flier to enter the race, held the women's transcontinental speed record. Still, no one thought Ingalls had a chance. Everyone knew this year's Bendix was a two-man race between Roscoe Turner and Benny Howard, head-to-head once again.

Even Louise's husband, Herb, believed the race would come down to Turner and Howard. Herb wasn't doubting Louise. He was just an engineer running the numbers. At best, he told Louise, she might finish third and take home the women's prize—if she could beat Earhart.

Earhart's new Lockheed Electra was four times more expensive than the Beechcraft waiting for Thaden in Wichita. And it was loaded with features: twin engines, retractable landing gear, and enough gas reserves to fly nonstop for forty-five hundred miles. Maybe, they said, Earhart's Bendix entry was a warm-up for a flight around the world—a suggestion that Earhart denied from her new home in Los Angeles.

Across town, just a few miles away, Roscoe Turner was ready to beat Howard. And everyone said his plane was faster than ever before—"sensationally fast," one person declared.

In Chicago, Howard was ready too—and so was his speedy plane. *Mister Mulligan* was not just a machine; it was, by the summer of 1936, a legend. Children bought model kits to build their

Mister Mulligan, Benny Howard's plane, swept the 1935 air races and was the heavy favorite to carry Howard to victory again in 1936. *Smithsonian National Air and Space Museum (NASM 0056879)*

Thaden before the 1936 air races, at the controls of her borrowed Beechcraft, a plane she described as a "trim, blue princess." *Thaden Family Collection*

own miniature *Mister Mulligan*s, and aviation experts believed the plane to be unstoppable.

Thaden knew what she was up against. Earhart, for starters, and then Turner and Howard. Herb was probably right; third place would be great. But when reporters talking to Thaden suggested as much, it sounded like an insult, and Thaden refused to let it pass. She wasn't trying to win the "women's division," she declared, because, after all, there was no such thing. She was thinking bigger.

"We are going to fly in the Bendix," Thaden told reporters, "and unless some of the other pilots do better flying or show better speed, we will win it."

With that, Thaden climbed into the blue Beechcraft, pointed its nose into the hard prairie wind, and pushed east. She was heading for the starting line in New York City.

CHAPTER 34

SPLINTERS AND A GREASE SPOT

*E*arhart was already on the ground at Floyd Bennett Field in Brooklyn when Thaden and Noyes arrived. Her new Lockheed had performed well in its first long trip. Earhart was thrilled to announce that her plane had flown the last leg of the journey—Cleveland to New York—in just two hours and twenty-five minutes.

That time sounded good until Benny Howard blew into Brooklyn, along with his wife, Maxine, in *Mister Mulligan*. Just for fun, the couple had made the trip from Chicago to New York in a record-breaking two hours and forty-five minutes—proof that *Mister Mulligan* was still the fastest plane in America. Airfields on both ends of the continent were abuzz with excitement. And in Los Angeles, Vincent Bendix and Henderson headed out to Mines Field to await the pilots soon to be screaming in from New York: Howard and Earhart and Thaden. But in a stunning development, there would be no Roscoe Turner.

The Hollywood showman had problems with his plane long

before reaching the starting line in New York. In Burbank the week before the race, Turner could barely get the airship off the ground. Finally, with just a few days to spare, mechanics pronounced Turner's plane good, and he took off before dawn the next morning. But three hours into his journey to the starting line in New York, the throttle cut out, jiggling in his large hand, disconnected and worthless. As the plane began losing altitude, Turner, who had never crashed in nineteen years of flying, began looking for a place to make a forced landing amid the jagged canyons in western New Mexico. Malpais, locals called it. Bad country.

Turner had a parachute on his back, and he could have used it. But he hated the idea of parting with his beautiful golden plane. So despite the risks, Turner came in for a crash landing in the middle of nowhere at around ninety miles an hour.

On impact, the plane bounced fifteen feet in the air and began to cartwheel across the desert, flipping, snapping in half, and skidding to a halt.

Turner was only slightly injured—a miracle. But the nearest city was sixty-five miles away; the nearest Native American settlement, the Zuni reservation, eighteen miles. He climbed out of the wreckage and began to walk, hoping to find help. It was three hours before he stumbled upon a Zuni farmer with a couple of horses. It was several more hours before the two of them finally arrived at the reservation on horseback. And finally that night, more than thirteen hours after takeoff, Turner reached a telephone in New Mexico. He wanted to call his wife back in Hollywood to let her know he was alive. But he sounded nervous, like a different man.

"I'm pretty shaky," he admitted.

Roscoe Turner was returning to Los Angeles by train, leaving the wreckage of his golden plane in the desert. A pile of metal and wood.

"Splinters and a grease spot," Turner said. "It's a wonder I'm not too."

CHAPTER 35
GOODBYE, DARLING

*T*haden's six-year-old son, Bill, had been praying at bedtime. Every night, for the past few weeks, the same prayer: "Bless Mother," the little boy said, "and please let her pass all the others in the race . . . Bless Mother, and please let her pass all the others in the race . . . Bless Mother . . ."

Even with Turner out, few people thought Thaden had a chance to win the Bendix. It was Howard's race now. And if not Howard, then perhaps one of the other men: Joe Jacobson; George Pomeroy; or Buster Warner, a navy lieutenant with a crew of three men flying with him.

The night before departure, the pilots gathered at ten thirty for a final meeting at the airfield in Brooklyn. The meeting room there was small, and Thaden was distracted, thinking about the weather. Some of the other fliers had private weather services giving them reports, but not Thaden. She had only the ten-thirty advisory handed out to everyone that promised "generally good" conditions at least as far as Wichita, Kansas. Walter Beech was waiting for her there; he'd help Thaden refuel the plane halfway across the country. Olive Ann was in Los Angeles at Henderson's finish line. Thaden and Noyes tried to sleep. Then planes began roaring into the air.

Buster Warner, with his crew of three, got off first at 1:37 a.m. George Pomeroy took off next, followed by Earhart with her copilot, Helen Richey, in her new Lockheed, and then Joe Jacobson, the young flier determined to defeat Benny Howard. Jacobson was so confident of success that he was prepared to leave Brooklyn with a parachute that he hadn't checked or repacked in six months—a dangerous plan, which the airport manager overruled. They broke into a private plane in the middle of the night, stole a newly packed parachute, and gave it to Jacobson, who—ready now—waved to photographers in the moonlight and bounded into the sky, heading west.

Finally, after 5:30 a.m., Thaden and Noyes walked toward their blue plane on the airfield beneath the morning stars.

Most race fans had gone home by then, leaving just a few hundred people on the ground. But Herb was still there, standing by his wife's plane. "Goodbye, darling," Louise told him. "And try not to worry about us, will you?"

An old friend was there too: Ruth Nichols. She was still recovering from her plane crash in Upstate New York months earlier. But race officials had asked her to help out on the ground. Always loyal, never bitter, she had agreed.

"Good luck," she told Thaden.

Now, close to 6:00 a.m., Thaden angled the nose of her blue plane into the wind near a wall of race officials—timers and starters—at the end of the runway.

At exactly 5:56 a.m., the starter dropped his handkerchief. The timers hit their stopwatches. And Thaden and Noyes's plane sped down the runway and took to the sky just as the sun began creeping over the eastern horizon. Benny Howard and his wife, Maxine, were soon in the air, too, chasing Thaden's Beechcraft with *Mister Mulligan*. Then, just minutes later, the Howards' plane rocketed past the women. Thaden and Noyes had barely left New York, and they were already falling behind.

Mister Mulligan was flying 245 miles per hour and gaining on all of its competitors. Pomeroy's plane was slow. Warner's airship was too. And Earhart struggled to make good time due to other problems. Shortly after takeoff, the hatch over her head inside the cockpit blew open, nearly sucking out Earhart and her copilot. By Earhart's estimation, they lost forty minutes fighting the hatch before finally tying it down with a rag—the best they could do. They limped into Kansas City, their one refueling stop, trailing Howard by almost two hours. They then lost still more time, another twenty-three minutes, waiting for mechanics to wire down the busted hatch. Meanwhile, back East, it was beginning to look like Herb was right. Third place might be the best Thaden could do. Howard and Jacobson were simply too fast, with Jacobson the first to arrive in Kansas City.

The morning skies there were stormy. But Jacobson knew

this territory; Kansas City was his home. And, taking off, the flier quickly guided his plane to an altitude of six thousand feet. Suddenly, the left wing ripped away; it just folded back on the fuselage, causing an explosion that tore the plane to pieces. Jacobson was falling now—blown not only from the plane but somehow from his safety belt and his seat. He pulled the ripcord on his stolen parachute just in time. But even with the chute open, he was coming down fast, too fast, and looking like he might touch down in the fiery wreckage of his own plane. It was only the wind that saved him—a summer breeze blew him away from the flames at the last moment. And, somehow, Jacobson survived. But he was out of the Bendix, clearing the skies for one man.

CHAPTER 36
SKY GHOSTS

*B*enny Howard was thrilled by his time into Kansas City. He was definitely on pace to break Turner's record. "Everything's lovely," Howard reported on the ground in Kansas City, refueling *Mister Mulligan* and then returning to the air. He headed southwest in a straight shot for the finish line, fourteen hundred miles away, at Mines Field in Los Angeles.

The Howards should have been there no later than midday. But one o'clock came and went—and there was no white plane in the sky. The opening ceremonies started, and no Howard. He was late, people thought. Maybe lost. It was actually much worse. The overdue *Mister Mulligan* was still six hundred miles east, somewhere in western New Mexico's *malpaís*.

Benny, in the cockpit, was the first to notice a problem: a vibration in the plane's propeller. Something was wrong. He leaned forward to get a better listen when, without warning, one of *Mister Mulligan*'s propeller blades snapped and broke. Benny, caught by surprise, slammed his head inside the cockpit, cutting himself over one eye. Blood was everywhere. And the plane was spinning, following the lone propeller blade around and around, until the engine died and Benny regained control of the airplane. Then, together with his wife, he flew on in silence.

Like Turner less than a week earlier, the Howards now had two options. They could bail out and parachute to safety. Or they could stay with the plane and make a crash landing—on flat ground, if they could find it.

The Howards, like Turner, chose to land. Benny thought he saw a dry creek bed. But as they got closer to the ground, Benny realized this creek was actually a shallow lake. "No place to land," Benny said. He swung the plane around, hoping to land near one of the small streams feeding into the lake. But it was too late. *Mister Mulligan* was crashing.

The plane bounced and settled, plowing into bushes and rocks that knocked off the landing gear, crushed the nose of the plane, and pushed the engine into the cockpit. When *Mister Mulligan* finally came to a stop, Benny and his wife were alive but trapped under the engine—with broken bones in their legs and feet.

Both Benny and Maxine lost consciousness, waking sometime later in the worst possible situation. They were covered in gasoline and forty miles from the nearest town, but stuck inside the plane and unable to walk or move. They were going to die there, Benny figured. Then they spotted him: a Navajo man—a Native American from a nearby reservation—just standing there, looking at the Howards in silence.

They cried for help. He did not come. They screamed, and the man just walked around the plane. Finally, they wrote a note and somehow convinced the man to take it. He delivered it to a nearby trading post. But instead of help, the Howards just got more spectators—a dozen more Navajo afraid to approach the plane. One of them had seen the plane come down, and it worried him. *Sky chindi*, they called the couple who had fallen from the heavens. Sky ghosts.

For almost three hours, the Navajo just stood there watching, while Benny raged inside the cockpit. Finally, townsfolk arrived from Crownpoint, New Mexico, bringing axes to free the Howards and pickup trucks to drive them to the nearest hospital. They would survive. But Benny would lose his left leg. Doctors had to **amputate** it in order to save his life. And it would be a month before he and Maxine were well enough to go home to Chicago. The race, for them, was over.

CHAPTER 37

A WOMAN COULDN'T WIN

*B*efore takeoff, Thaden had worried about crashing like the Howards. She knew it was possible, and she tried to talk to Noyes about it back in Brooklyn.

"Blanche," Thaden said, "are you awake?"

"Yeah," Noyes replied, "are you?"

As the pilot, Thaden wanted Noyes to know that in the event of a problem, she would stay with the controls while Noyes parachuted to safety. "It's to be understood," Thaden said, "that you jump first."

Noyes wouldn't hear of it. "You have two children," she told Thaden, "so *you* jump first."

They left it like that, undecided and, hopefully, not necessary. Still, it had been worth discussing. Thaden knew anything could happen in the Bendix, and by morning, a couple of hours out of New York, she was already staring down the first problem. Her blue Beechcraft was lost somewhere over the Allegheny Mountains. A thick fog blanketed everything. And the plane's radio had been reduced to static—"useless," Thaden called it—making it impossible for the two women to check their position. Finally, after ninety minutes, they broke clear of the fog and began scanning the ground for a landmark or, even better, an air-marker.

"Look!" Noyes said finally, spotting a sign.

Thaden guided the plane down to four thousand feet and circled. The sign was indeed an air-marker. Noyes used it to fix their position. "We are only ten miles off course!" she shouted a moment later, pounding Thaden on the back. The women were on track. But they lost time near St. Louis, fighting storms and crosswinds. "Tighten your belt," Thaden told Noyes. And when they reached Wichita, Walter Beech was upset at their time.

"What do you think you're in?" he asked Thaden, meeting her amid the fuel trucks on the airfield. "A potato race?"

He and the women had no way to know what had happened to the Howards in New Mexico. And until they landed in Wichita, Thaden and Noyes couldn't have known about Joe Jacobson exploding in the skies over Kansas or about Earhart's blown hatch tied down by a rag. Regardless, Beech didn't think Thaden was going fast enough, and he begged her to fly harder.

"Open this thing up," he demanded.

"Yes, sir," Thaden told Beech.

But really, she wasn't listening. It might have been seven years since the Powder Puff Derby, but she remembered why she had won that race: by not getting lost, by not rushing and making mistakes, and by not burning out the engine by flying too fast. She took off in Wichita after an eleven-minute stop—she and Noyes hadn't even gotten out of their seats—and flew west into the storms, the rains, and the headwinds fighting them all the way to California.

The two women did not speak of winning the Bendix. They just flew: over the flatlands where Thaden had gotten her start selling coal and the mountains that the men had once warned were too dangerous for female pilots to cross; over the deserts where Turner had crashed and the Howards had, too, and the *malpais* that had claimed the lives of so many other aviators.

They flew for Marvel Crosson, who'd died in 1929, and for Ruth Nichols, who had nearly died too many times to count in deserts and forests and flames. They flew for Florence Klingensmith, who gave her life in Chicago, and for Frances Marsalis, killed while racing in Dayton, desperate to win that thousand dollars but getting no credit for her efforts, only blame. And they flew for the others who had paid a price over the years: the missing Frances Grayson, her secrets held by the sea; the insulted Ruth Elder, her secrets known by all; Olive Ann Beech, waiting in Los Angeles; and Thaden's son, Bill, with his prayers in Bentonville. It was almost 6:00 p.m. in Los Angeles when the little blue plane appeared in the eastern sky, coming in low and fast. They had arrived in Los Angeles, crossing the continent in fourteen hours and fifty-five minutes—slower than Roscoe Turner's record, yes, but a new female record.

As the Beechcraft taxied across the field, race officials began running along next to it, hollering nonsense, it seemed to the two women in the cockpit. "I wonder what we've done wrong now," Thaden said to Noyes.

Then, after the plane rolled to a stop, Henderson stepped up.

"I'm afraid you've won the Bendix," he said.

Thaden didn't believe him at first. But, climbing out onto the wing, she and Noyes soon realized that maybe it was true. They could see it in the photographers pushing toward them, flashbulbs firing. They could see it in Henderson's face and they saw it, too, in the eyes of Olive Ann Beech, pressing forward to greet them on the ground. She was fighting back tears as she threw her arms around Thaden, pulled her close, found the words she was seeking, and spoke them into her ear.

"So," Beech said, "a woman couldn't win, eh?"

—————

Thaden had beaten her nearest competitor, Laura Ingalls, by almost forty-five minutes, the closest man by fifty minutes, and Earhart, in her expensive Lockheed, by almost two hours. In doing so, she claimed more than nine thousand dollars in winnings— seven thousand dollars for first place and twenty-five hundred for being the first woman to land. Vincent Bendix personally signed the check for the woman's prize while telegrams began pouring in, congratulating Thaden on her victory.

"Congratulations from your home town."

"You deserve the honor."

"All Arkansans are proud of you."

Thaden collected the massive Bendix Trophy. She gave a

speech she could hardly remember, and then she traveled by police escort downtown, where an aviators' ball was about to begin at the Ambassador Hotel.

But somewhere in the night, Thaden slipped away. There was something she needed to do. She found a Western Union office and prepared to send a telegram of her own to her mother and kids back in Bentonville.

There were so many things Thaden could have said, so many stories to tell. But it was almost midnight back in Arkansas. The kids were surely asleep, and Thaden decided to keep the telegram short.

"We won," she wrote, and left it at that.

PART IV

CHAPTER 38

DISAPPOINTMENTS, DEDICATION, AND COURAGE

*T*he story of Thaden's victory in the Bendix made headlines that week in every major American publication: *Newsweek, Time* magazine, the *New York Times,* the *Los Angeles Times,* the *Chicago Tribune,* and almost every other newspaper, large or small, from coast to coast. But the women on the ground in Los Angeles were the first to cheer Thaden for winning—and the first to jab Henderson about it too.

"At last, the races have gone feminine," one woman told him.

"More power to the women," another informed Henderson.

"Ladies first!" said still another.

They hadn't forgotten the past or the rules that had once banned them from racing. And, together, the women celebrated. Earhart was especially pleased. With Thaden's victory, she predicted a day in the near future when men and women would stand as equals, judged not by their gender but by their abilities. "If a woman wishes to enter important competitions," Earhart told reporters, "the question will be, 'Is she a good enough flier?' instead of primarily a matter of whether she wears skirts or trousers." That's all the women had ever wanted, and now they had proof they could compete if only they had the chance.

Thaden went on tour, posing for photos, giving interviews, signing autographs, and collecting her Bendix Trophy from Vincent Bendix himself. More important, Thaden's win in the race paved the way for other women. Two years later, in 1938, Jacqueline Cochran won the Bendix race in a time almost seven hours faster than Thaden's. Had Thaden and the other women failed in 1936, Cochran might never have gotten that chance. From the beginning, all the women had been connected, whether they liked it or not, building on one another's successes, saddled with one another's failures, and pressing on together. As Earhart said once, the women had to keep fighting, keep knocking on the door, if they ever wanted to be accepted in this male-dominated world. "As more knock," Earhart explained, "more will enter."

———

Earhart wasn't worried about her poor finish in the Bendix. She and Putnam were already turning their focus to her still-secret around-the-world flight.

In January 1937, four months after the Bendix race, she finally announced her plans. She would leave California that spring, she said, flying roughly twenty-seven thousand miles and making stops, at times, at small refueling points—like Howland Island, a speck of sand in the middle of the Pacific Ocean.

To find it, experts said, a pilot would have to be perfect. And for that reason, Earhart was glad to be making the trip with navigator Harry Manning. Without him, she felt she'd be unable to find a place as small as Howland Island.

Thaden didn't like the idea, and that February she told Earhart as much.

"You have nothing to gain," Thaden said, "and everything to lose."

It was a quiet moment away from the press, inside Earhart's hangar in California. The two friends were sitting on the side of an inflatable raft that would be part of Earhart's emergency supplies.

But Earhart just smiled, squeezing Thaden's hand. Thaden squeezed back, and the two women stood up to say goodbye, wisecracking to break the tension. They began joking about Earhart's funeral.

"If I don't see you before you shove off for Hawaii," Thaden said, "what flowers should we send?"

"Water lilies seem appropriate, don't you think?" Earhart joked.

She understood the risks. Still, she was going. "Women," she explained, "must try to do things as men have tried. Where they fail, their failure must be but a challenge to others."

The failures for Earhart began almost immediately. After making a successful hop from Oakland to Honolulu in March 1937—with Manning; a second navigator, Fred Noonan; and Paul Mantz on board, assisting with the flying—Earhart crashed her Lockheed while trying to leave Hawaii. She was headed back to California—by boat.

Two months later, Earhart was ready to go again, with just a few changes to the plan. She would be flying this time with only Fred Noonan; Harry Manning was out. They would be going east, not west, to adjust for seasonal changes in global weather. And they would be leaving over the objections of not just friends like Thaden but government officials who wanted to stop her.

For a month, she and Noonan seemed to prove the skeptics wrong. They traveled some twenty-two thousand miles, jumping from Oakland to Miami, Brazil to Senegal, Sudan to India, Burma to Australia, and finally to Lae, New Guinea. Next stop: Howland Island, 2,556 miles to the east.

The trip would last almost twenty hours with no land in sight most of the way. To make it, Earhart and Noonan would fly through the day and night and into the next dawn. And then they'd have to make radio contact with a U.S. Coast Guard ship named the *Itasca* waiting off the shore of Howland Island. Early on the morning of July 2, the *Itasca*'s radio operator, Leo Bellarts, began hearing from Earhart in a series of reports.

"About 200 miles out," she said at 5:15 a.m.

"About 100 miles out," she said thirty minutes later.

And then, at 7:30, a problem: "We must be on you," Earhart reported to the *Itasca*, "but cannot see you. Gas is running low. Have been unable to reach you by radio. We are flying at 1,000 feet."

Outside, the sky was blue; a pilot could have seen for almost twenty miles. And Earhart believed she had to be close to Howland Island.

"But cannot see island," she reported. "Cannot hear you."

"Earhart calling *Itasca* . . ."

At 8:44 a.m., Bellarts heard from Earhart one last time. Her tone, firm and tense an hour earlier, was now frantic; desperate, even. "That of a frightened woman," Bellarts thought, "in a voice close to breaking."

He never heard from her again.

The U.S. Navy immediately launched the largest search it had ever conducted. Three thousand people in 102 airplanes and ten ships combed roughly 250,000 square miles of ocean—a search area the size of Texas. But they never found Earhart, Noonan, or their plane, and on July 18, after more than two weeks of searching, they finally gave up and went home.

Earhart was gone. Just where or how, no one could ever say for sure. More than eighty years later, her disappearance remains a mystery. Reporters still write stories speculating about what might have happened to Earhart—and some people are still searching for her plane in the Pacific Ocean. But in the quest to learn how she died, we seem to have forgotten both how she lived and the lives of the other women who flew with her.

Each woman's story had its own unique ending.

———

Ruth Nichols once promised that she would keep going "wherever the air trail leads"—and she did that. In 1958, at the age of fifty-six, she flew a U.S. Air Force supersonic jet at speeds exceeding a thousand miles an hour nearly six miles above the Earth—a feat no woman, even Earhart, could have imagined two decades earlier. Nichols boldly declared that women would have a future in space exploration. Women, she said, were better suited than men to be astronauts, being calm in emergencies, with "a greater ability than men to summon up their forces to meet a challenge." And she also predicted that she would be among the first female space pilots. "When spaceships take off," she said, "I shall be flying them."

Nichols was half right, as it turned out. Women would indeed go to space—American astronaut Sally Ride flew on the space shuttle *Challenger* in 1983. But Nichols wouldn't survive to see either accomplishment. Nichols was struggling, and had been for a long time. She felt like a failure.

It wasn't just because of her plane crashes or her bad luck. It was because she couldn't get hired in aviation. In the 1930s and '40s, Nichols applied to be a pilot, copilot, or employee at almost every single major airline. With most male pilots off at war, Nichols was sure she was qualified to fly. Yet the airlines had no interest in hiring her. They didn't want to hire women. It would be 1973 before major U.S. airlines began recruiting women to be pilots.

With nowhere to go, no flying jobs for her, Nichols began working in the public relations office of a hospital in White Plains, New York. It wasn't what she wanted. But in the late 1950s, Nichols finally caught a lucky break. A publisher agreed to print her book about her career in aviation—*Wings for Life,* she called it. Within three years, Ruth Nichols was dead. She was just fifty-nine.

⸻

Ruth Elder struggled too, quickly losing her fame and her money.

Life got so hard for Elder that by 1950 she even changed her name to hide from the world. She was now calling herself Susan Thackeray and living with George Thackeray, her fifth husband, in San Diego. This marriage—like the others before it—didn't last. And soon Elder was divorced again. But near the end of her life, she found love with one of her ex-husbands—Ralph King, a Hollywood cameraman.

She was finally happy, it seemed, living with King in San Francisco, and content, maybe for the first time, to just be herself: Ruth Elder, for better or worse, with her feet on the ground.

"Flying in the sky is nice," she said at age seventy-three in 1976, "but the earth has so many wonderful things in it to make people happy."

Elder died in her sleep fifteen months later, slipping away without any farewells. She had prepared for this moment, at least, telling her husband how to handle her remains: Ruth Elder wished to be cremated and have her ashes scattered from an airplane into the sea.

⸻

"Disappointments," Thaden said with a sigh late in life. For the female pilots along the way, there were so many of them. The women knew what the men thought of them, and it was hard, at times, to keep going, to keep flying. "It took dedication," Thaden explained. "And the courage to accept defeat, after defeat, after defeat."

Thaden thought a lot about Nichols and about the other female pilots who struggled after their time in the sky was over. She stayed in touch with many of them, actually. But then, Thaden stayed in touch with almost everyone from the time of the air races—with Cliff Henderson, with Olive Ann Beech, with Blanche Noyes.

Henderson retired from the air races to build a town in the California desert. Olive Ann turned Beechcraft into one of the largest aviation manufacturers in America. And Noyes worked for decades as an air-marker for the government. Pilots were thankful for Noyes—and they were thankful for Thaden, too. Into 1937, they cheered her at aviation shows and named her the best female pilot in America.

Then, in June 1937, one week before Earhart disappeared, Thaden made a sudden announcement: she was quitting aviation, retiring at the peak of her fame. she knew what she was giving up. But she wanted to be with her kids, to really know them. Take them to the beach in summer. Go sledding with them in winter. And even teach them how to fly.

In 1950, Thaden and her daughter, Patsy, flew in a revival of the Powder Puff Derby, flying in a borrowed plane from Montreal to West Palm Beach, Florida. The Thaden women finished third. But it was Thaden's son, Bill, who really took after his mother, growing

Thaden wanted to spend time with her children, Bill and Patsy, and would ultimately make a difficult choice. *Thaden Family Collection*

up to serve in the U.S. Air Force and then working as a pilot for Eastern Airlines.

She and Herb lived the last two decades of their lives in High Point, North Carolina. Herb died in early 1969, and Louise kept going, living just long enough to be rediscovered. In 1976, the airport in Bentonville was rededicated Louise Thaden Field. And the governor in Arkansas declared that Sunday "Louise Thaden Day." Still, the news of Thaden's death a few years later, just before her seventy-fourth birthday in 1979, didn't travel far. It was ignored by the national newspapers that had once followed her everywhere. By walking away from racing at the height of her popularity, Thaden had pulled off a vanishing act of her own.

But she didn't regret it. Thaden was satisfied with the life she had lived and the decisions she had made.

"I have never been far away, nor will I ever," she told Patsy once. And nothing, not even her death, could change that. "Will you remember that—always?" Thaden asked her daughter. "Wherever I am, I will be with you."

She would be, she said, in the rustling of the leaves on the trees and the lazy drift of the clouds across the sky. She would be in the whispers on the wind, in the great blue horizon, and in the falling rain.

"The sunset will be a part of me," Thaden said, "and the smell of flowers in the air."

All her children had to do, she said, was close their eyes, and they would find her. They would feel her presence in the air.

Glossary

AERONAUTICAL: relating to the science of making and flying aircraft

ALLIED: the nations that fought together against Germany during World War I and World War II

ALTITUDE: the height of an object in relation to sea level

AMPUTATE: to remove a limb, typically by surgery

AVIATION: the flying or operating of aircraft

BOYCOTT: to refuse to buy, go into, or participate in something in order to bring about change

BRACE WIRES: wires that help support the wings when a plane is in flight

BREADLINES: lines in which people stand to receive food from the government or a charity

BUCKLE: to bend or fall apart

CHRISTEN: to give a name to or dedicate something

COCKPIT: the area from which a pilot controls an airplane

CORONER: a public official who investigates a death that may not have occurred from natural causes

DISENGAGE: to release or detach something

DURALUMIN: a hard but light metal made primarily of aluminum and copper

ENDORSEMENT: money earned from recommending a product or person

EXPLOIT: a bold or daring feat

FEMINISM: the belief that men and women should be treated equally and given equal opportunities

FOLLY: a lack of good sense or judgment

FUSELAGE: the body of an airplane, to which the wings, tail, and engines are attached

GRIT: toughness of character

GRUDGE: a deeply held feeling of anger

HANGAR: a shelter for aircraft

HORSEPOWER: a unit of power equal to 746 watts, or 550 foot-pounds of work per second

HULL: the main body of an aircraft or ship

INQUEST: an official inquiry or examination, especially in front of a jury

INVESTORS: people or companies who put money into something in order to make more money

NAVIGATE: to steer or control the course of something

NAVY DESTROYER: a small, fast warship

NOTORIOUS: to be known for something negative

PHILOSOPHER: a person who studies the nature of life, truth, and knowledge

PONTOONS: a float used on the bottom of a seaplane

PUBLICITY: information given to the media that gets attention from the public

PYLONS: towers that may be used as points of reference for airplanes, or as turning points in a race

RAMBUNCTIOUS: behavior that is wild and difficult to control

REGULATE: to control via a set of rules

RUDDER: a moveable blade at the rear of an airship used to control direction

SCHOONER: a sailing ship with at least two masts

SEAPLANE: an airplane that takes off from and lands on water

SEXTANT: a tool used for navigating according to the positions of the stars

SINGLE-PROPELLER PLANE: a plane with just one engine

SOCIALITE: a person who is prominent in fashionable social circles

TENT CITIES: a collection of tents set up in an area to provide shelter for people, usually the homeless or temporarily displaced

THROTTLE: a device that controls the amount of fuel flowing into an engine.

TOXIC: containing a poisonous material that could cause death

TRANSATLANTIC: going across the Atlantic Ocean

TURBULENCE: unsteady movement in the sky caused by winds, air
pressure, or temperature changes

TYCOON: an influential and powerful businessperson

TYPHOID FEVER: a disease marked by fever, diarrhea, and headache,
usually caused by bacteria

WIRE: to send word by telegraph

Source Notes

Abbreviations Used in Notes

AE	Amelia Earhart
AOE	Amy Otis Earhart
FK	Florence Klingensmith
GPP	George Palmer Putnam
LT	Louise Thaden
PTW	Pat Thaden Webb
RN	Ruth Nichols

AS	*Anniston Star*
BG	*Boston Globe*
CITP	Muriel Earhart Morrissey, *Courage Is the Price* (Wichita, KS: McCormick-Armstrong, 1963)
CPD	*Cleveland Plain Dealer*
CSM	*Christian Science Monitor*
FOI	Amelia Earhart, *The Fun of It* (Chicago: Academy Chicago Publishers, 1932)
"FWTF"	Cliff Henderson, "From Wasteland to Fairyland"

	(unpublished manuscript, date unknown, given to the author by Cathy Scott, Henderson's stepdaughter)
HWF	Louise Thaden, *High, Wide and Frightened* (Fayetteville: University of Arkansas Press, 2004)
LAT	*Los Angeles Times*
"LITHW"	Janet Mabie, "Lady in the High Wind" (unpublished manuscript, Schlesinger Library, Harvard University)
NYDN	*New York Daily News*
NYHT	*New York Herald Tribune*
NYT	*New York Times*
OT	*Oakland Tribune*
PEE	*Portland Evening Express* (Maine)
PP	*Pittsburgh Press*
PPH	*Portland Press Herald* (Maine)
"STF"	Louise Thaden, "So They Flew" (unpublished manuscript, LTC, box 4, NASM)
WB	*Wichita Beacon*
WE	*Wichita Eagle*
WFL	Ruth Nichols, *Wings for Life* (Philadelphia: J. B. Lippincott, 1957)
20 Hrs.	Amelia Earhart, *20 Hrs., 40 Min.* (Washington, D.C.: National Geographic Society, 2003)
CHC	Cliff Henderson Collection
FKC	Florence Klingensmith Collection
HCSCC	Historical and Cultural Society of Clay County

HSPD	Historical Society of Palm Desert
IWASM	International Women's Air and Space Museum
LTC	Louise Thaden Collection
NASM	Smithsonian National Air and Space Museum
RNC	Ruth Nichols Collection
SHLA	Springfield History Library and Archives
SLRC	Schlesinger Library, Radcliffe College
USC	University of Southern California
WEIU	Women's Educational and Industrial Union
WIAA	Women's International Aeronautic Association
WOABC	Walter and Olive Ann Beech Collection

Introduction

1   *"In such a crisis . . . or you die"*: Paul Collins, *Tales of an Old Air-Faring Man* (Madison: University of Wisconsin Foundation Press, 1983), 65.

2   *"Many pilots have . . . wood fuselage ships"*: Bertram W. Downs, *The Modern Airplane* (St. Paul, MN: Roth-Downs Airways, 1928), 59.

"It has become . . . the World Series": CHC; HSPD; miscellaneous race clippings.

4   *colorful planes*: Ninety-Nines Museum, *Women in Aviation* 42 (July 20, 1930).

Chapter 1: The Miracle of Wichita

7   *"was a follower of boyish pursuits"*: "Beautiful Wichita Girl Flies! And How! Sells Travel Airs," *Wichita Evening Eagle*, December 31, 1927.

8   *on his long car trips*: "Former Bentonville Girl Wins Fame By Sale of Commercial Planes in California," *Arkansas Gazette*, September 4, 1927.

"Write, stating age . . . where last employed": "Help Wanted—Female," *WE*, June 30, 1927.

as early as 1922: "Should Women Draw the Same Pay as Men?,"
Wichita Beacon Sunday Magazine, November 12, 1922.

"Everything in Coal": WB, October 28, 1921.

"Coal Is Scarce . . . Coal Bin Now": "To Wichita Coal Users," advertisement in Ibid., August 11, 1917.

9   *"I want to stay . . . me to stay"*: "$30,000 Airplane Factory," WE,
     August 22, 1926.

     two airplane factories: "Wichita a City of Air Fans," WE, August 12,
     1926.

     Ford Reliability Tour: "Beech in Travel Air Wins Second Reliability
     Tour," *Aviation*, August 30, 1926, and "Navigating the Airplane Reli-
     ability Tour," *Aviation*, September 6, 1926.

     "Don't save this . . . win the race": "Great Epic of the Air," WE, Octo-
     ber 3, 1926.

10   *"It's certainly good . . . hard, fast flying"*: "Beech Makes Average of
     128 MPH on Wichita Hop," WE, August 14, 1926.

     hit a man on the ground: "Beech Winner of Ford Tour," *Wichita Sun-
     day Beacon*, August 22, 1926.

"Let us consider . . . them to accomplish": "Great Epic of the Air," WE, October 3, 1926.

11   *McPhetridge once jumped*: "A Girl Flies to Fame," *Pacific Flier: Magazine of Air Commerce,* n.d., box 1, NASM, LTC.

drove her father's car: Some stories say she began driving at age nine, others say eight; box 1, news clippings, NASM, LTC.

"Warren has agreed . . . how to fly": HWF, 12.

12   *"Oh, Louise"*: HWF, 12.

"It is . . . thing I want to do": "Beautiful Wichita Girl Flies!"

April 1927: HWF, 13.

almost freezing: "Weather," WE, April 2, 1927.

Chapter 2: Devotedly, Ruth

13   *no street number*: The official address for the Nichols family, according to U.S. Census records, was 275 Grace Church Street, but in all of Nichols's correspondence, she listed no number, just the street name.

dark and scary: Nichols's nephew Norman Nichols, interview with the author.

three of them: New York State Census, 1925.

14   *a wealthy man with social connections*: In her memoir *Wings for Life*, page 22, Nichols wrote that she was not following "the prescribed course for a delicately reared sub-deb."

Did she have . . . her own life?: Ibid., 36.

her eighteenth birthday: Résumé and biographical details, RNC, IWASM.

Every fiber: Nichols wrote in *WFL* that she climbed into the plane with "a feeling of panic," 16.

five foot five: Résumé and biographical details, RNC, IWASM.

"I felt . . . my earthly body": WFL, 19.

"College life . . . great!": Letter home from Nichols dated September 29 [1919], Family Correspondence, 1919–1921, RNC, IWASM.

15 *"Devotedly, Ruth"*: Ibid., letter home from Nichols dated September 29 [1919].

mother and father pressured her: WFL, 23.

"How much are . . . dollars an hour": Ibid., 24.

to pay Rogers five hundred dollars: Ibid., 25.

"For Pete's sake . . . I tell you!": Ibid., 31.

"dumb . . . numbskull speed": Ibid., 30.

16 *"I'm a flier now . . . make it yet"*: Ibid.

in the fall of 1922: Wellesley College records relating to Ruth Nichols.

Chapter 3: An Extremely Interesting Girl

17 *"I want to fly . . . teach me?"*: Neta Snook Southern, *I Taught Amelia to Fly* (New York: Vantage Press, 1974), 101.

one inch at a time: Ibid., 112.

renting out rooms: Ibid.

lessons on credit: Ibid., 102.

18   *"I want to . . . whenever I can":* CITP, 128.

for about two thousand dollars: George Putnam and Earhart's sister, Muriel, later wrote that the plane cost just five hundred dollars. But in her first memoir, written in 1928, Earhart said it was two thousand (*20 Hrs.,* 22).

"All in all . . . for a beginner": Southern, *I Taught Amelia to Fly,* 122.

Twice, she and Earhart crashed: Both Southern and Earhart wrote about these crashes, with different details, in their respective memoirs.

"We have to look . . . the reporters come": Ibid.

in air rodeos: "Pasadena Air Rodeo," *Ace,* December 1921, 7.

falling in love: Earhart herself almost never spoke of Sam, but her sister recounts what she knew of their relationship in her memoir, and Sam himself spoke about it to reporters from the *Medford Mercury.*

tall and redheaded: "Inter ting Sidelights on Big Welcome to Flyers," *Medford Mercury,* July 13, 1928.

19   *"A Lady's Plane . . . KINNER AIRSTER":* advertisement, *Ace,* June 1922.

Airster had been sold: 20 Hrs., 32.

"In the near future . . . indeed": "Reporter Learns That Amelia Has Sweetheart," *Medford Mercury,* June 8, 1928.

20 *kept a scrapbook:* AOE Papers, SLRC.

dropped out of Columbia University: Columbia University records.

"owing to financial difficulties": AE, letter to friend, October 1925, Marian Stabler Collection, IWASM.

August 18, 1926: WEIU files, SLRC.

21 *"anything connected . . . aeronautical concern":* Ibid.

five foot eight: LT interview, 1971, PTW Family Files.

"An extremely interesting . . . does write": WEIU files, SLRC.

"Holds a sky pilot's license?": Ibid.

neighborhood was filled: Boston City Directory and ward 3, plate 14, Norman B. Leventhal Map Center, Boston Public Library.

22 *"When I leave . . . never go back"*: AE, letter to friend, October 1925, Marian Stabler Collection, IWASM.

Chapter 4: The Fortune of the Air

23 *"Gentlemen . . . Raymond Orteig"*: "Puts Up $25,000 for Paris Flight," *NYT*, May 30, 1919.

"And see what you can do": Biographical details about Orteig's early life come from the obituary "Raymond Orteig, Hotel Man, Dies," *NYT*, June 8, 1939.

24 *"This flight . . . if it succeeds"*: "Fonck to Fly American Plane Across the Atlantic," *NYHT*, March 31, 1926.

"Dashed to pieces . . . alive": "Wings of Uncertainty," *NYT*, February 20, 1927.

25 *in a blue uniform*: Fonck's flight and failure were covered by the national press, including these detailed accounts: "Fonck Plane Burns, Two Die, at Start of Paris Flight, Ace and Curtin Escape," *NYT*, September 22, 1926; "Two Die When Fonck's Plane Falls in Flames," *BG*, September 21, 1926; and "Fonck's Plane Burned, 2 Die, But He Plans to Try Again," *NYHT*, September 22, 1926.

26 *"Warmest congratulations . . . of French aviation"*: "How the Airmen Arrived," *Guardian,* May 10, 1927.

27 *"We'll see you soon"*: The details of Nungesser's flight and takeoff can be found in a number of places, among them "Nungesser and Coli Missing in Atlantic Flight Attempt," *Aviation,* May 16, 1927; "Nungesser Off on Paris–New York Hop," *NYT,* May 8, 1927; "Davids of the Air Brave Goliath of Elements," *NYHT,* May 9, 1927; and "Nungesser Flying Over the Atlantic Hops Off at 5:19 A.M.," *NYHT,* May 8, 1927.

a celebration at the Hotel Astor: "Throng to Greet Nungesser at Battery Today," *NYHT,* May 9, 1927.

28 *"My prayers will save him"*: "Nungesser Seen Leaving Ireland, British Assert," *NYHT,* May 11, 1927.

"Are you only taking . . . any more, either": Russell Owen, "Lindbergh Leaves New York at 7:52 A.M.," *NYT,* May 21, 1927.

29 *"Ready, Slim . . . Ready"*: Ibid.

At a boxing match: "44,000 Join in Prayer That Lindbergh Wins," *NYT,* May 21, 1927.

30 *"Defeat and death . . . at it unafraid"*: Owen, "Lindbergh Leaves New York."

"Awaiting Lindbergh . . . darn nice boy": Lindbergh sound files, San Diego Air and Space Museum.

31 *"I feel a lot lighter . . . in the heart"*: "Raymond Orteig, Hotel Man, Dies."

Chapter 5: The Fairest of the Brave and the Bravest of the Fair

33 *barely flying anymore*: FOI, 57.

34 *"Gas bought . . . back for me"*: "Girl, 23, Flies Here for Paris Jump Sunday," *NYHT*, September 15, 1927.

35 *"Perfectly powdered"*: "Miss Elder Insists on Flight to Paris," *Philadelphia Inquirer*, September 15, 1927.

"What is this . . . fly to Paris": "Smile of Ruth Elder Causes Many Guesses on Her Flight," *AS*, September 22, 1927.

"I'm here to . . . Quickly": "Girl, 23, Flies Here for Paris Jump Sunday."

36   *"The fairest of . . . of the fair"*: Picture caption, *Defiance, Ohio, Crescent News*, September 14, 1927.

"I've lived for a while . . . Yes, it is": "Explaining Ruth Elder," *BG*, November 30, 1927.

37   *"Please keep my plans . . . is in aviation"*: Letter from Frances Grayson to Harry Jones, Harmon Museum and Old Orchard Beach Historical Society, Old Orchard Beach, Maine.

"We are not . . . into the 'movies'": "Two Women Plan Overseas Air Expedition," *NYHT*, September 3, 1927.

"I would rather give . . . and do less": "Will Fly from Paris to New York," *Muncie Evening Press*, September 7, 1927.

"Flying Matron": "Flying Matron Plans Hop to Maine Today," *NYDN*, October 8, 1927.

38   *sold two million dollars*: "Frances Grayson Sacrificed a $2,000,000 Realty Business to Make 'Safe and Sane' Flight," *Brooklyn Daily Eagle*, December 27, 1927.

give her thirty-eight thousand dollars: "Will Fly from Paris to New York."

S-36 Flying Boat: "The New Sikorsky Flying Boat," *Aviation*, September 5, 1927.

"Don't worry . . . going to fail": Ibid.

"I am . . . child of destiny": International News Service, "Fulfillment of Dreams Near, Says Mrs. Grayson," October 15, 1927.

"American women believe . . . my marriage": "Miss Elder Up in Tests Today for Her License," *NYHT*, September 17, 1927.

39   *"I'm no bluffer or faker"*: Ibid.

chunk of wing . . . and a wheel: "Old Glory Dived Head On in Sea, Wreck Indicates," *NYHT*, September 22, 1927.

"fine young men": "Hoover Adverse to Flight Ban as Unfair to Youth," *NYHT*, September 11, 1927.

40   *"It is rather useless . . . purpose in mind"*: "Lindbergh Talks Generally on Sea Hops—Silent on Elder Attempt," *NYT*, October 12, 1927.

41   *"They shall not stop me"*: "Ruth Elder Has Been Flyer but Two Years," *BG*, October 12, 1927.

Chapter 6: The Lion's Cage

42   *morning of Elder and Haldeman's departure*: Most details of Elder's takeoff from New York come from two accounts: "Flapper Wings for Paris," *NYDN*, October 12, 1927, and "Ruth Elder Takes Off on Paris Flight, Soars with Haldeman into Ocean Dusk," *NYHT*, October 12, 1927.

     "*Ruth ribbon*": "Miss Elder Trailed by Throng at Field," *NYT*, September 19, 1927.

44   *In the cockpit*: The details about Elder and Haldeman's flight over the ocean in the rest of this section come primarily from Elder's four-part, first-person account, published that fall in the *AS* and other newspapers under the headline "Ruth Tells of Atlantic Flight." Additional details related to the SS *Barendrecht* saving Elder and Haldeman come from the ship captain's own first-person account via the United Press story published around the world on October 15, 1927.

45   "*the hazard of the enterprise*": "The Dawn Due to Hop Thursday," *PPH*, October 12, 1927.

46   "*This is a pioneer flight*": "The Dawn Takes Off from Curtiss Field," *PPH*, October 11, 1927.

going broke: "Mrs. Grayson's Entire Fortune Used Up on Fateful Ocean Flight; Wouldn't Cancel Attempt Because of Duty to Money Backer," *Brooklyn Daily Eagle*, January 8, 1928.

"I wish her Godspeed . . . enough for both": "Flapper Wings for Paris."

"Congratulations . . . prayers followed you": "Grayson Plane Escapes Storm, Starts Today," *NYHT*, October 14, 1927.

47   *"Gray fog . . . almost November"*: In October 1927, while stuck in Old Orchard Beach, Grayson wrote a pondering letter that reads almost like a diary entry. She gave it to a *NYT* reporter, saying he could publish it "if something happen[ed]" to her; "'Still Small Voice' Led Mrs. Grayson," *NYT*, December 26, 1927.

Snow was already falling: "Snowfall at Moosehead Proves Aid to Hunters," *PPH*, October 25, 1927.

48   *what might have happened*: Reports of various radio messages swept up and down the U.S. coast and through the Canadian maritime provinces for days after the *Dawn* went missing. Accounts of these reports can be found in the following articles, among others: "Five Destroyers to Continue Hunt for Missing Plane," *PPH*, December 29, 1927; "Dirigible Back at Hangar After 31 Hours' Vain Hunt," *PEE*, December 28, 1927; "'Plane Down—Can't Last Long'; Mystery

Message Upsets Island," *PPH*, December 30, 1927; and "Plane Heard Late Saturday Evening Over Newfoundland," *PPH*, December 30, 1927.

"Built to float for two weeks": "Father Fears for Safety," *Muncie Evening Press*, December 24, 1927.

last radio message: Several reports placed the *Dawn* over Cape Cod around 7:30 the night it went missing; see "Dawn Crew Plunged to Death Off Cape Cod in Howling Storm," *PEE*, January 2, 1928; "Last Known Dispatch," *PEE*, December 29, 1927; and "Mrs. Grayson and the Dawn Heard from by Radio," *PPH*, December 25, 1927.

49   *"But she was . . . overrode our objections"*: Associated Press, December 24, 1927.

"There she is . . . l'American Girl": Details of Elder's arrival in Paris can be found in the following stories: "Thousands Greet Miss Elder as Plane Arrives in Paris," *NYT*, October 29, 1927; "Paris Welcomes Ruth Elder and Aid as Sky Conquerors," *NYHT*, October 29, 1927; and "Throngs at Paris Greet Ruth Elder," *BG*, October 29, 1927.

2,623 miles: "Flew 2,623 Miles, New Oversea Record," *NYT*, October 14, 1927.

four hundred thousand dollars: "Coolidge Presents Medal to Lindbergh; 6,000 See Ceremony," *NYT*, November 15, 1927.

"Ruth Elder Day": The details about Elder's homecoming come from the *AS*'s coverage of the events in the following stories: "Anniston Expects Huge Crowd Ruth Elder Day," December 19, 1927; "Hometown Gives Ruth Big Reception," December 20; "Ruth Elder Resting Today After Hectic Welcome Activities," December 21, 1927; "City Prepares to Bid Famous Guests Goodbye," December 22, 1927; "Kiwanis Club Honors Ruth and Haldeman," December 22, 1927; "Ruth Elder, Haldeman Depart from Anniston After Three-Day Visit," December 23, 1927; and "Dinner Party at Club for Miss Elder," December 25, 1927.

50 *"the Happy . . . American Midinette"*: "Throngs at Paris Greet Ruth Elder."

"Ace-high housekeeper . . . in her glory": Stories of Womack's frustration about his wife's exploits and their ultimate divorce can be found in multiple papers in 1927 and 1928, including "Ruth Elder's Mate Bars Flying," *NYHT*, November 5, 1927; "Mate and Aunt Here at 'Outs' to Greet Miss Elder," *NYHT*, November 8, 1927; "Curious Throngs Greet Ruth Elder Mid Sirens' Blast," *Brooklyn Daily Eagle*, November 11, 1927; "Return to Dishes? No, Vows Ruth," *OT*, November 12, 1927; "Ruth Elder's Husband Charges Cruelty in Suit," *NYHT*, September 7, 1928.

"*The nation will hope . . . the lion's cage*": "Today," AS, October 15, 1927.

"*She showed courage . . . Ruth Elders*": "Women Criticize Elder Attempt," NYT, October 14, 1927.

Chapter 7: Flying Salesgirls

52   *How could she escape?*: WFL, 41.

"*I would not . . . foolhardy*": "Women Criticize Elder Attempt," NYT, October 14, 1927.

53   "*Want to come . . . do we start?*": WFL, 42.

headed to Rockaway: Ibid.

before 8:00 a.m.: Flight log of the journey was published in detail in the *Miami Herald* under the headline "Log of New York–Miami Flight," January 6, 1928.

54   "*Please . . . personal things*": "Woman Passenger on Miami Flight Evades Limelight," *Miami Herald*, January 6, 1928.

"*I have always . . . way to travel*": Ibid.

"*Only a wee bit . . . like a rooster*": "Athletic Accomplishments," loose in book, in Ibid.

55   *her grit:* "'Round San Francisco Bay," *Western Flying* (June 1928).

twenty-nine million: "Woman Vote Plays Big Part This Year," *NYT*,
July 9, 1928.

"I don't see . . . they sell airplanes?": "Oakland Girl Sells Planes," *OT*,
January 12, 1928.

56   *knew what he wanted:* "The Thaden 'Argonaut,'" *Aviation*, February
13, 1928.

57   *invited one person:* "Local Girl Aviatrix Weds Captain Vo. Thaden."

change McPhetridge: Pat Thaden Webb, interview by the author.

headed to the sanitarium too: Thaden's crash with William A. "Sandy"
Sanders was covered in detail in Bay Area newspapers, including
the following stories in the *OT*: "Probe Is Begun of Plane Crash
that Hurt One Man," March 14, 1928; "Alameda County Has First
Flying Deputy," July 6, 1927; "Aerial Officer Himself Jailed," July
8, 1927; "Aerial Officer Forfeits Bail on Drunk Charge," July 15,
1927; "Oakland Flier Killed in Crash," August 20, 1928; "Planes to
Soar Over Rites for Oakland Flier," August 21, 1928; "Coroner's
Jury Finds Death Accidental," August 28, 1928. Additional details
related to the overheating engine and Thaden's feelings about the
crash come from her memoir *HWF*, 25, 27.

58 *got married in Reno*: "Oakland Aviatrix Weds Plane Designer."

"Gosh . . . stay too long": Herb Thaden, letter to Louise, July 25, 1928, PTW Family Files.

Chapter 8: The Right Sort of Girl

59 *"right sort . . . good breeding"*: Hilton Howell Railey, *Touch'd with Madness* (New York: Carrick and Evans, 1938), 101.

60 *"George Palmer Putnam . . . wear shadows well"*: "Reminiscences of GPP," GPP Papers, Purdue University.

"Pull your chair . . . all you can": Putnam and Railey each have different recollections of how they learned about the *Friendship* flight and who was in charge of finding a woman to replace Guest, and they each render their dialogue about it with different phrasings. Earhart, too, has slightly different phrasings of the conversations she had with Railey. But overall, the sentiment is the same. The exchanges rendered here between Putnam and Railey come from Railey's account in his memoir *Touch'd with Madness*, 100.

61 *"The stories of . . . hard to believe"*: "Big Swindles Bared in Alien Smuggling," *NYT*, June 29, 1925.

English classes for new immigrants: 20 Hrs., xxii.

around their tables: "Interview in South End Kitchen Where She Often Sat," *BG*, July 11, 1937.

62   *"Because your picture . . . for some time"*: Letter from Earhart to Nichols, September 15, 1927, AE Papers, Purdue University.

"Flying is still . . . more women flying": "When Women Go Aloft," *Bostonian* (May 1928).

63   *"Call Denison House . . . for Amelia Earhart"*: Railey, *Touch'd with Madness*, 101.

children ran around: FOI, 58.

"You don't know . . . H. H. Railey": Ibid., 59.

"I might as well . . . fly the Atlantic?": Ibid.

as mechanic: GPP, "Lady with Wings: The Life Story of my Wife Amelia Earhart," *Liberty*, n.d., AE Papers, SLRC.

the second meeting: The best descriptions of Earhart's meeting in New York come from three places: *20 Hrs.*, 42; "Lady with Wings"; and *CITP*, 141–42.

"a crisis": *20 Hrs.*, 42.

"too fascinating": Ibid.

64　*be average*: CITP, 141.

"Didn't offer to . . . fare home, either": Ibid., 142.

"Why do you . . . ride a horse?": Mabie interviewed Amy Guest's lawyer, David T. Layman, in 1944, who recalled for her his meeting with Earhart; the story is recounted in "LITHW," vol. 9, 7a.

65　*"I'll be back . . . summer school"*: "Lady with Wings."

rumors were starting: Boston Evening Transcript, June 4, 1928.

high-laced boots: "LITHW," vol. 9, 15.

"It is . . . 50–50 bet": "Lindbergh's Success," PEE, October 26, 1927.

"Hooray for the . . . was worthwhile, anyway": AOE Papers, SLRC.

66　*the flight was troubled*: 20 Hrs., 54, and AE, flight log, Seaver Center in Western History Research, Los Angeles County Museum of Natural History.

five tons: FOI, 64.

into the sea: This near disaster is recounted in multiple places, including *20 Hrs.*, 53, and AE, flight log.

"I do not know . . . selected this port": F. Burnham Gill, "First Woman to Cross the Atlantic in a Flying Boat," *Newfoundland Quarterly* 60, no. 4 (Winter 1961–62).

"What in the . . . you doing here?": "LITHW," vol. 10, 3.

67　*"What is in store . . . this trap"*: AE, flight log.

"We're going today . . . spite of everything": Details of takeoff in Trepassey come from "Monoplane Friendship Lands Safely," *St. John's Evening Telegram*, June 18, 1928; "LITHW," vol. 10, 7; and Gill, "First Woman to Cross the Atlantic."

68　*one last time*: "Monoplane Friendship Lands Safely."

Forty miles an . . . Sixty: FOI, 73, and "Lady with Wings."

Chapter 9: Where Is Miss Earhart Now?

69　*"Many hours to go . . . like water"*: AE, flight log.

"Where is Miss Earhart . . . coming back soon?": *20 Hrs.*, xxiv.

70   *"Two boats . . . Why?"*: AE, flight log.

"Well, that's out": "Miss Earhart Predicts Great Airport at Trepassey for Transocean Flights," *NYT*, June 21, 1928.

a "mess": AE, flight log.

two hundred and fifty thousand people: "Boston Shouts Joy to Amelia Earhart," *NYT*, July 10, 1928.

two thousand social workers: "Big Throng of Women at Reception in Hotel," *BG*, July 10, 1928.

greatest celebration: "Thousands Pay Tribute to the Friendship Flyers," *Medford Mercury*, July 13, 1928.

Chapman too weak: CITP, 135.

72   *"all-right girl"*: "Miss Earhart's Homecoming," *NYHT*, July 8, 1928.

"The best-known . . . a little lady": These quotes about Earhart come from multiple sources including "Miss Earhart's Smile and Poise Capture Huge Throngs in Boston," *BG*, July 10, 1928; "Miss Earhart Feted, Companions Beg Off," *BG*, June 21, 1928; and "Secret Flight

Miss Earhart's Original Plan," *Brooklyn Daily Eagle*, June 10, 1928.

"What's the matter . . . sack of potatoes": "Chance Sent Amelia Earhart on First Ocean Venture," *Philadelphia Evening Bulletin*, September 10, 1938.

"She might well . . . gasoline supply": "What Has Miss Earhart's Flight Accomplished?," *Boston Traveler*, July 8, 1928.

Chapter 10: City of Destiny

75   *popular kids*: Education folder, CHC, HSPD.

FREE AIRPLANE . . . EACH USED CAR: "FWTF," 94.

77   *twenty thousand dollars in debt*: "FWTF," 101.

ten more in nearby towns: Aeronautical Chamber of Commerce of America, *Aircraft Year Book*, 1928, 162.

78   *downtown Los Angeles*: Mines Field site-selection papers, March 16, 1928, LAX historical archives, Flight Path Museum.

"Line up, gentlemen . . . Grasp it!": "Why Local Airfield Is Choice," May 29, 1928, race scrapbook, CHC, Purdue University.

79   *two hundred thousand dollars in prizes*: "Elaborate Plans for Air Exposition," *NYT*, September 9, 1928; "Program Fixed for Air Races," *LAT*, August 5, 1928.

three hundred thousand watched for free: "City Declared Flying Center," *LAT*, September 17, 1928.

thirty thousand frightened fans: "Air Stunt Hero Hurt in Crash," *LAT*, September 11, 1928.

missing only one thing: Ruth Elder and Amelia Earhart were both invited to the 1928 races; Elder flew some sort of exhibition but did not race. Earhart didn't fly at all.

one of his stages: "FWTF," 112.

Chapter 11: If This Is to Be a Derby

80   *Famous Fliers*: "Notables of Air Due at Dance," *LAT*, September 13, 1928.

81   *busted plane*: "Plane Fixed, Miss Earhart Hops for West," *Pittsburgh Post-Gazette*, September 3, 1928.

"I am just an amateur": "Miss Earhart Flies to Town," *LAT*, September 14, 1928.

the crowds below: LTC, NASM.

"I am not a good pilot": "Five Miles Up," *Motormates,* December 1928.

82 *"You must be very careful":* HWF, 19.

to think about anything: "Woman Finds High Flight Is Safe, Irksome," OT, December 11, 1928.

83 *she rose above the fog:* "Five Miles Up."

"All world's aviation . . . women pilots": "Woman Finds High Flight Is Safe, Irksome."

"Well, I made it . . . I'm tired": "Woman Flier Breaks Record," OT, March 18, 1929.

84 *"World's Leading Woman Flier":* San Francisco Examiner, March 27, 1929.

a big success: "Thaden Concern Sold to Pittsburgh Group," *Aviation,* February 16, 1929.

"No more . . . sensational flying": "Fair Pilot Holding Two Records Living Here," PP, April 28, 1929.

85 *"Our objective . . . women in aviation"*: Ibid.

"You are no . . . Cleveland air races?": Letter from McQueen, February 18, 1929, WIAA, USC.

"I see no . . . Los Angeles airports": Letter from Earhart to McQueen, undated WIAA, USC.

86 *"would be too . . . on the ladies"*: Ibid.

"pink tea affair": Letter from Thaden, May 18, 1929, WIAA, USC.

"If this is to . . . the aeronautical world": Ibid.

"If we can't . . . trying to ride?": "Women Fliers Balk at Easy $10,000 Race; Don't Want Men's Aid in Flying over Rockies," *NYT*, June 12, 1929.

87 *strike a compromise*: "No Men to Fly with Women in First Air Race," *CSM*, July 15, 1929.

Chapter 12: There Is Only One Cleveland

88 *bouncing checks*: Letter to Nichols from Curtiss Flying Service, dated August 6, 1929, folder BU-05, RNC, IWASM.

89   *about her age:* According to U.S. Census records for the Crosson family, Marvel was her given name.

"Marvel Crosson . . . sure winner": Santa Monica Evening Outlook, August 18, 1929.

"I have given . . . in the world": "Tragic Air Death Forecast in Article by Miss Crosson," *San Diego Union,* August 30, 1929.

two weeks after Crosson: According to the *Wichita Eagle,* Marvel left Wichita bound for Los Angeles on July 27; according to the *LA Times,* Thaden left Wichita on August 13.

was blue: "Mrs. Thaden Is Derby Victor," *CPD,* August 27, 1929.

flawed from the start: HWF, 45.

was to begin: "More Women in Air Race," *LAT,* August 14, 1929.

forced landings: Nichols recounts the forced landings in *WFL,* 80; newspapers in Wichita, El Paso, and New York also covered the events.

90 *walk for miles*: "Motor Sent Ruth Nichols, Forced Down in Arizona,"
    NYHT, August 17, 1929.

    "Come on out here, Louise": Fox Movietone newsreel, August 1929,
    Moving Image Research Collection, University of South Carolina
    Libraries.

    "There is only . . . Find it": "STF," 2.

Chapter 13: Beware of Sabotage

91 *turn to take off*: "STF," 4.

    "The men . . . have been foolish": "Miss Earhart Says Derby Must Be
    Safe," *Santa Monica Evening Outlook*, August 15, 1929.

92 *"One hundred percent . . . unduly careful"*: Letter from Thaden, April
    8, 1929, WIAA, USC.

    "Good luck, old girl": "STF," 3.

94 *"the she derby"*: Will Rogers, syndicated columns, August 19 and
    August 20, 1929.

    as previously planned: "Derby Fliers Ban Calexico as Stop Point,"
    San Bernardino County Sun, August 19, 1929.

"Beware of sabotage": Pilot Thea Rasche received this telegram and shared it with the press, who ran stories of it across the country.

95   *"Gas . . . everything"*: "Women Derby Fliers Reach City," *Arizona Republican*, August 20, 1929.

      "Stall it in . . . all make it": "STF," 9.

96   *"Well, yes, there is"*: This and other quotes about the flight to Phoenix come from Ibid., 9.

      seven thousand people: "Women Derby Fliers Reach City."

97   *"Marvel Crosson . . . in the mountains"*: HWF, 50.

      eyewitness accounts: "Famous Women Fliers Are Honored Guests at Exchange Club Banquet," *Arizona Republican*, August 20, 1929.

Chapter 14: No Time to Stop

99   *"They snapped . . . cut by pliers"*: *San Bernardino County Sun*, August 21, 1929.

      "I must have . . . flying in circles": "Women Derby Fliers Reach City."

"Women are lacking . . . men possess": "Women Indignant at Effort of Oklahoma Man to Halt Derby," WE, August 24, 1929.

"For the present . . . confined to men": Arthur Brisbane, nationally syndicated column, August 21, 1929.

100 *"This is no time to stop"*: "Women Indignant at Effort of Oklahoma Man to Halt Derby."

"Who is this . . . on our abilities?": "Girls Peeved," PP, August 25, 1929.

101 *on day six*: Details of the city's preparations come from the WE in the following stories: "Night Turned into Day as Huge Beacon Light Floods Port," August 20, 1929; "Dinner Dance for Women Fliers Will Be Big Affair Here," August 21, 1929; "Plans Completed for City's Welcome of Derbyists," August 23, 1929; and "Program at a Glance," August 23, 1929.

"the daily battle . . . precious minutes": "STF," 26.

"Atta baby . . . didn't you?": Ibid., 28.

"Knight of the Air": "For Five Years Beech Has Been Smashing Records as a Wichita Aviator," box 3, WOABC, Wichita State University Libraries.

"You keep on . . . win the race": Details here from Thaden's race from Wichita to Columbus come from her unpublished memoir "STF."

105 *"a squashed beetle"*: WFL, 92.

"I'm awfully glad . . . could have won": The details of Thaden's arrival in Cleveland come from multiple papers on August 27, 1929, including the *Cleveland News,* the *Cleveland Press,* Thaden's first-person account published in the *WE,* "Dedicate Cup to Memory of Sister Flier," and the *CPD*'s detailed coverage in two different stories, "Mrs. Thaden Tells Own Story of How She Won Derby Race" and "Mrs. Thaden Is Derby Victor."

106 *"If it hadn't . . . leading now"*: "Nerves Growing Taut," WE, August 25, 1929.

"I haven't . . . I'm sorry": "Flying Colonel Gets His Privacy," *CPD,* August 27, 1929.

107 *$4,600*: Tabulated from news accounts in the *CPD* and *Pittsburgh Post-Gazette.*

earned in 1929: Statistical Abstract of the United States, 1930, table no. 368, "Average Weekly and Hourly Earnings: All Wage Earners and Classified Groups of Labor, 25 Manufacturing Industries." The chart shows that women in these fields made, on average, $17.62

per week, a little more than $916 per year. Even when accounting for the fact that an office manager might make $20 a week, Thaden's winnings dwarfed a woman's average earnings in 1929.

talk it over: There are varying accounts about who came up with the idea to form an organization and when. The idea dates back to at least 1927, when Earhart first suggested the plan to Ruth Nichols, and other women had similar plans. What's clear is that the idea was discussed under the trees at the air races in Cleveland. Recollections from Gladys O'Donnell, August 24, 1965, Gladys O'Donnell Collection, IWASM.

Chapter 15: Good Eggs

108 *Six hundred thousand people:* "Air Races Succeed Financially; 600,000 See Events at Port," *Cleveland News,* September 3, 1929.

almost 9,500: Aeronautical Chamber of Commerce of America, *Aircraft Year Book,* 1929.

more planes in 1929 . . . in American history: Aeronautical Chamber of Commerce of America, *Aircraft Year Book,* 1929.

"Without women . . . future for aviation": "Sky Pilots—Feminine Gender," *Independent Woman,* April 1929.

109 *"decoration"*: "Lady Mary Heath Tells Women's Aid to Flying," *Detroit Free Press*, April 5, 1929.

"helpless . . . catty about her": "Women and Aviation," *Flying*, December 1929.

around a bigger issue: Women in Aviation 10 (November 19, 1929).

110 *"for all licensed girl pilots"*: Letter from female pilot and original Ninety-Niner Opal Kunz, December 31, 1929, Ninety-Nines Museum.

"Her strength . . . amazing": LT, *Air Facts*, July 1970, LTC, NASM.

111 *By January 1930*: The Aviation column in the *Pittsburgh Post-Gazette*, on January 31, 1930, written by Thaden, mentioned that ten women were currently enrolled, and according to other local stories, at least three others had enrolled in the fall of 1929.

112 *mishap in Harrisburg, Pennsylvania*: "Noted Aviatrix Nearly Crashes After Inspecting City Airport," *Harrisburg Evening News*, April 24, 1930.

113 *"Gosh, I'm anxious . . . something awful"*: Letter from Thaden to her parents, July 3, 1930, LTC, NASM.

"He's just . . . That's all": "Plane to be Cradle of Son Born to Flying Thadens," *PP*, July 31, 1930.

Chapter 16: Mr. Putnam

114   *"When and if . . . to Mr. Putnam"*: Earhart, letter to her mother, August 26, 1928, AOE Papers, SLRC.

115   *wasn't fond of him:* Louise Thaden interview, 1971, PTW Family Files.

      "If I were . . . no mystery of it": Associated Press, June 5, 1930.

116   *member of her family:* "Amelia Earhart Weds G. P. Putnam," *NYT*, February 8, 1931.

Chapter 17: Law of Fate

117   *"OBJECT . . . pilot of the ship"*: Planning for Around the World memo, 1928–30, RNC, folder FL-10, IWASM.

118   *in the Allegheny Mountains:* Accounts of Nichols's forced landing in Manns Choice, Pennsylvania, come from multiple sources, including *WFL*, 109; *HWF*, 136; "Noted Aviatrix Leaves Manns Choice Field," *Bedford Gazette,* November 27, 1930; "Aviatrix Forced Down," *Cincinnati Enquirer,* November 20, 1930; and part 5 of "Wings East," the five-part story of Nichols's life written by C. B. Allen and John

Forbes that appeared in the *New York World-Telegram* in June 1931.

119 *young girls:* These letters from the young girls and Nichols's replies can be found in Fan Mail, 1928–32, folder CN-05, RNC, IWASM.

120 *"Would you be . . . an Atlantic hop":* Letter from Ruth Nichols, March 21, 1931, RNC, IWASM.

121 *Money began rolling in:* Transatlantic Financing, folder FL-19, RNC, IWASM.

"Early in May . . . absolutely definite": Letter to Railey, folder BI-03, RNC, IWASM.

122 *"All right . . . help me":* The office dialogue between Nichols and Railey was reported by Allen and Forbes, "Wings East," part 5.

123 *"Definitely not . . . considered":* Telegram from Railey to Nichols, April 21, 1931, folder BI-03, RNC, IWASM.

to bring with her: Transatlantic Things to Take, folder FL-25, RNC, IWASM.

"I'll see . . . other side!": Letter from Nichols to Railey, April 10, 1931, folder BI-03, RNC, IWASM.

Chapter 18: No In-Between

124 *"Please advise . . . London and Paris"*: Letter from Railey's secretary
to Nichols, May 22, 1931, folder BI-03, RNC, IWASM.

"to search, discover or explore": "Ruth Nichols Ready to Start on Sea
Flight," *NYHT*, June 14, 1931.

125 *"I guess the reason . . . in the world"*: Letter from Mildred Morgan to
Nicholas, May 3, 1931, in ibid.

Rockaway, Queens: Details about Nichols's flight come from multiple news sources on June 23, 1931, including the *NYT*, the *NYHT*,
the *Brooklyn Daily Eagle*, and the *New York World-Telegram*.

126 *in the middle*: Detailed accounts of Nichols's landing in New Brunswick can be found in the *NYT*, *NYHT*, and the *St. John Telegraph
Journal*, June 23 and June 24, 1931.

Get . . . out: WFL, 157.

127 *"Wire for another plane"*: "Injured Aviatrix Is Looking Forward to
Ocean Hop in Fall," *St. John Telegraph Journal*, June 24, 1931.

at least two bones in her back: In personal letters, Nichols wrote that
she'd broken four vertebrae. Doctors told newspapers it was two.

Chapter 19: The Man in the Mansion

128   *"The air race . . . this year's event"*: 1930 Air Races folder, CHC, HSPD.

    "They naturally . . . to kindergarten": "Women Flyers Kick at Rules for Air Races," *Chicago Tribune*, July 20, 1930.

129   *"selfishly exploiting us"*: Letter from Thaden, July 25, 1930, Ninety-Nines correspondence, folder GR-22, RNC, IWASM.

130   *awarded at an airplane race*: "$10,000 Posted for Air Races," *CPD*, June 1, 1930.

    flaming disasters: Coverage of the plane crashes and deaths at the 1930 races can be found in the *Chicago Tribune* and other Chicago daily newspapers on August 28, August 30, and September 2.

    barely made a profit: Proposal for the 1934 air races listing the financial figures for each previous year, CHC, NASM.

131   *Elm Court*: Chateau Bendix has been reborn today as the Trinity School at Greenlawn, a private school for students in grades seven through twelve. Tom Noe, director of the school's development office, gave me a tour of the estate in January 2017 and opened up the school's files on the old building, making this description possible.

132   *"But how . . . and where?"*: "FWTF," 8.

he got lucky: Ibid., 9.

in the club car: Don Dwiggins, *They Flew the Bendix Race* (Philadelphia: J. B. Lippincott, 1965), 13.

"Mr. Bendix . . . for some months": Dwiggins and Henderson each recount the same story of the meeting with slightly different dialogue. In this, I am relying on Henderson's version, "FWTF," 9.

Chapter 20: Give a Girl Credit

134   *"He's . . . Doolittle's coming!"*: "Sets New Trans-U.S. Flight Record," *CPD*, September 5, 1931.

135   *"furthering . . . aeronautical knowledge"*: Nichols, letter to Swanee Taylor, May 6, 1931, Transatlantic Press Coverage, folder FL-18, RNC, IWASM.

"sit back . . . notice": *Women in Aviation* 47 (September 21, 1930).

"There, little girl . . . what have you": Letter from someone who appears to be C. B. Allen, aviation editor at the *New York World-Telegram*, June 26, 1931, Transatlantic Press Coverage, folder FL-18, RNC, IWASM.

"If it was . . . might have happened": Correspondence between Nichols and Thaden, July 3 and July 6, 1931, Correspondence: Thaden, Louise, folder CN-11, RNC, IWASM.

136 *"You can do . . . get the money"*: "Ruth Nichols Bravely Faces Future Although Hurt; Visions City as Coming Air Terminus," *St. John Telegraph Journal,* and "Ruth Nichols Is Overjoyed with Assurance That 'Akita' Can be Reconditioned for Help," *St. John Telegraph Journal,* June 26, 1931.

loaned her money: Letter from Nichols, October 3, 1931, Transatlantic After Crash, folder FL-21, RNC, IWASM.

"The only record . . . miles non-stop": "Ruth Nichols Seeks Record," OT, October 22, 1931.

137 *By one a.m.*: "Ruth Nichols Lands Here, Claims Record," *Louisville Courier-Journal,* October 26, 1931.

by dawn: WFL, 192.

Chapter 21: Grudge Flight

139 *"gradually . . . public eye"*: Carl B. Allen, unpublished manuscript, "Ladybird in Revolt," 3, NASM.

"grudge flight": Ibid., 1.

140 *"Flying . . . with What?"*: "Ruth Nichols' Wings Clipped," *Inside Stuff*, February 20, 1932.

lunch in Rye: Accounts differ as to exactly which day Earhart and Nichols had lunch. What's clear is that it was right before Earhart left, which is confirmed by *WFL*, 209, and Allen, "Ladybird in Revolt."

141 *north for Canada*: Unless otherwise noted, all details concerning Earhart's 1932 transatlantic takeoff, flight, and landing come from the primary news accounts of the day in the *New York Times*, the *New York Herald Tribune*, and the *Boston Globe*, May 21 and May 22, 1932.

"Please . . . get there, eh?": Movietone footage, 1932, AE Papers, Purdue University.

"To all my . . . fifteen hours": Unless otherwise noted, all details concerning Earhart's 1932 transatlantic takeoff, flight, and landing come from the primary news accounts of the day in the *NYT*, the *NYHT*, and the *BG*, May 21 and May 22, 1932.

143 *"You beat me . . . a splendid job"*: Nichols's comments and others' congratulating Earhart come from 1932 Solo Transatlantic Flight, Post-Flight Correspondence, AE Papers, Purdue University.

144 *"This is the . . . suffrage in aviation"*: Ninety-Niner (February 1932), Ninety-Nines Museum Archives.

Chapter 22: *Spetakkel*

147 *"I want to go . . . possibly can"*: "City Aviatrix May Fly Ocean," *Minneapolis Star*, July 25, 1932.

148 *spetakkel*: Ingvald Stensland, interview with Mark Piehl, May 2, 1991, FKC, HCSCC.

found other hobbies: Ibid. and Moorhead High School yearbooks, 1921 and 1923.

for Lindbergh Day: Details of Lindbergh's visit to Fargo, including his arrival and the parade route, come from coverage in the *Fargo Forum*, August 25 and August 26, 1927.

just five foot four: Star Tribune, May 18, 1931.

149 *"Show him . . . these things, too"*: Ibid.

only a bathing suit: Minneapolis Journal article and photo, undated, FKC, HCSCC.

"It has been . . . ladder to climb": Ninety-Niner (September 15, 1933), Ninety-Ninety Museum Archives.

150 *"The men . . . against Florence Klingensmith"*: "Women Pilots
Compete with Men on Equal Terms for First Time in Races," *CPD*,
August 28, 1932.

Chapter 23: Anything You Want

151 *of the little plane*: Lowell Bayles pilot's license application at U.S.
Department of Commerce, Lowell R. Bayles Collection, SHLA.

152 *"Anything you want . . . feel no breeze"*: "Acrobatics—Sane and Asi-
nine," *Sportsman Pilot*, April 1931.

shooting star on a string: Witness report of Joseph Brandenburg,
December 7, 1931, Record Group 342, Airplane Accidents 1931–1932,
Department of Defense central files, National Archives, College
Park, Maryland.

153 *"To fly that . . . of one's finger"*: "Russell Boardman Victim of Fate,"
Indianapolis Star, July 6, 1933.

Chapter 24: Say Hello to the Crowd

154 *"No doubt you . . . let me know"*: Letter from Cliff to Florence Klin-
ginsmith [*sic*], August 14, 1933, CHC, HSPD.

"hopelessly . . . the race": "Turner Shatters Own Mark to Win Trans-
U.S. Derby," *Philadelphia Inquirer*, July 2, 1933.

155 *four hundred thousand visitors*: "Nearly 400,000 Expected for Weekend," *Chicago American*, July 2, 1933.

"Florence . . . hello to the crowd": "Death Stalks the Air Racers," *Popular Aviation* (March 1934).

156 *"Ah, but I . . . as any man"*: Ibid.

670 horsepower: There is some discrepancy in news reports and eyewitness interviews about the horsepower of the engine in Florence's borrowed Gee Bee. In news accounts, it is reported as 420. In interviews conducted by the coroner, it was reported to be 670. Either way, what's clear is that it was at least twice the horsepower of the engine intended for the plane, and perhaps bigger still.

157 *"Just look at . . . a beautiful race?"*: "Aviatrix Thought of Crowd's Safety Rather Than of Own," *Fargo Forum*, September 7, 1933.

Chapter 25: Her Life for the Show

158 *"I believe that . . . into a dive"*: This quote and others about the investigation into Klingensmith's crash come directly from the transcript of the coroner's inquest in Chicago; see Cook County Coroner Inquest transcript and report no. 456969, Cook County Criminal Court, September 5, 1933, FKC, HCSCC.

159 *"A Gee Bee . . . off the right wing"*: Cook County Coroner's Verdict,
September 5, 1933, FKC, HCSCC.

"wasn't well . . . weakened condition"': "Aviatrix, Ill, Met Death in
Proving Women Can Equal Men, Inquest Told," *Chicago Daily News,*
September 5, 1933.

well attended: Details about Florence's funeral come from the *Minneapolis Journal,* September 11, 1933, and "Dozen Pilots Here Today
in Last Tribute to Girl Flier," *Fargo Forum,* September 7, 1933.

160 *"in many cases . . . property and life"*: Memo to air bureau director
Gene Vidal, November 29, 1933, Record Group 40, box 570, U.S.
Department of Commerce central files, National Archives.

"Miss Florence Klingensmith's . . . I already knew": "Should Women
Race Planes?," *CSM,* January 16, 1935.

Chapter 26: All Things Being Equal

162 *"It's over, gal . . . going to land"*: "Famous Woman Flier Tells Experi-
ences of Record Flight," *WB,* December 19, 1932.

163 *"Torn between two loves"*: HWF, p.92.

"Pat to you!": Birth announcement, September 1933, PTW Family
Files.

"who died proving . . . basis with men": Ninety-Niner (September 15, 1933), Ninety-Nines Museum.

mailed surveys: All quotes and details regarding the employment surveys sent out in 1933 come directly from the surveys themselves saved for decades by Ruth Nichols and kept in 99s Labor Questionnaire, folder GR-25, IWASM.

164 *"I want to warn . . . almost impossible"*: Nichols mentioned her concerns on this front in many letters over the years. This quote comes from a letter to fellow pilot Thea Rasche, General Letters, folder CB-10, RNC, IWASM.

165 *to give a speech*: Letter from Ruth Nichols, October 24, 1929, Lectures Correspondence, folder AU-05, RNC, IWASM.

to get fifty dollars: Schedule of fees, Lectures Material 1933–37, folder AU-08, RNC, IWASM.

"A long over-water . . . news flight left": Letter to Powel Crosley, October 17, 1933, Potential Sponsor Rejection, folder BU-15, RNC, IWASM.

Chapter 27: Men Pilots Only

166 *three hundred dollars to appear*: "A $300 Talk," *Des Moines Register*, October 19, 1933.

"It is coming . . . building this evening": "Large Crowd for Amelia Earhart," *Emporia Gazette*, October 14, 1933.

167 *"When a man . . . when a girl does"*: Helen Welshimer, "Fly, Girls, Fly," nationally syndicated column, July 1932.

"Women . . . differently from men": Associated Press, November 10, 1933.

"Obviously . . . this decision": "Banning of Women Pilots in New Orleans Races Revives Equal Rights Controversy," *NYHT*, February 4, 1934.

169 *blue-and-yellow Gee Bee*: News clippings, Gee Bee Airplanes, vol. 4, SHLA.

170 *show didn't last long*: The details about the mishaps in New Orleans come from "Stunt Flier Meets Fiery Death in Fall Before Grandstand," *New Orleans Times-Picayune*, February 15, 1934, and "Aviator and Jumper Killed as Airplane Plunges into Lake," *New Orleans Times-Picayune*, February 18, 1934.

Chapter 28: That's What I Think of Wives Flying

171 *"The '99' girls . . . as contestants"*: Cooper letter to NAA secretary W. R. Enyart, July 27, 1934, Jacqueline Cochran Papers, box 2, A76-4,

1934 Correspondence, Dwight D. Eisenhower Library, Abilene, Kansas.

"If any individual . . . of all types": Cliff Henderson, letter to Cooper, August 3, 1934, Jacqueline Cochran Papers, box 2, A76-4, 1934 Correspondence, Dwight D. Eisenhower Library, Abilene, Kansas.

172 *"And boy . . . that $1,000"*: "Flyer Had Laugh About Fatal Last Lap on Race," *Dayton Daily News,* August 6, 1934.

173 *one by one*: Accounts of the crash come from the next day's detailed news coverage in two local newspapers, the *Dayton Daily News* and the *Dayton Journal,* August 6, 1934.

stunned: HWF, 96.

"When my time . . . one grand splurge": Ibid., 97.

174 *"Everyone knows . . . theory is right"*: "Fair Fliers Wrathy Over Racing Ban," *Akron Beacon Journal,* August 24, 1934.

"Flying . . . man's business": "Women Flyers on Sidelines, 'Don't Like It,'" *Cleveland News,* September 1, 1934.

"I do not believe . . . quite agree": "Speed Pilot's Wife Sees Woman's Place on Ground," *Cleveland Press,* September 3, 1934.

"*Imagine a jockey's . . . wives flying*": "Women Flyers on Sidelines, 'Don't Like It.'"

175 "*I've half . . . to get killed*": "Doug Davis, Air Winner, Killed in Trophy Race Crash, 100,000 Watch," *CPD*, September 4, 1934.

two-man race: The details about Davis's fatal race come from the daily news coverage in three newspapers, the *CPD*, the *Cleveland News*, and the *Cleveland Press*, on September 4, 1934.

177 "*It's a wonder . . . racing pilots killed*": "Ask Longer Race Course Due to Davis Death," *Cleveland News*, September 4, 1934.

Chapter 29: An Excellent Type of Woman

178 "*Two capital Ts . . . other, Tradition*": Changing Standards, Fourth Annual *New York Herald Tribune* Conference on Current Problems, 1934, speech transcript, William Brown Meloney papers, Columbia University Rare Book and Manuscript Library.

"*Her place . . . aptitude places her*": "Aviatrix Arrives After 'Longest Ride on Train,'" *Minneapolis Star*, November 30, 1934.

179 "*Cliff Henderson . . . the Clock*": Ninety-Niner (August 1934), Ninety-Nines Museum.

"Women have . . . as men have": "Women Aviators Honor Memory of Mrs. Marsalis," *NYDN*, August 7, 1934.

"Be it resolved . . . foundation whatsoever": Ninety-Nines resolution, signed by president Margaret Cooper, September 1934, Ninety-Nines Museum.

180 *voted to support*: "Aviation Editors Want Women on Race Program," *CPD*, September 4, 1934.

Just after Christmas: Details of Earhart's solo Pacific flight in this section come from the following sources: Purdue University Special Collections, scrapbook #12; *Honolulu Advertiser* and other clippings; and the *OT* news coverage of her arrival on January 12 and January 13, 1935.

twenty-four hundred miles: "Throngs Cheer Perfect Hop Across Pacific," *OT*, January 13, 1935.

"There is nothing . . . land plane": "Earhart Plan for Solo Hop Opposed Here," *Honolulu Star-Bulletin*, December 29, 1934.

Chapter 30: They'll Be in Our Hair

183 *"It is my . . . they keep trying"*: Letter from Turner to Ruth Osgood, October 9, 1935, box 30, folder 1, Roscoe Turner Collection, University of Wyoming American Heritage Center.

"I wouldn't let her": Ben Howard, oral history, 1960, 44, Columbia University Special Collections.

184 *"The women . . . foreground of the picture"*: "Women Fliers 'Muscle In' at Races; Win Major Roles in National Show," *Cincinnati Enquirer*, August 25, 1935.

"The first thing . . . and become pests": "Pilots Suggest Ban on Women Flyers at Races," *CPD*, September 4, 1935.

races began in Cleveland: "Women Fliers 'Muscle In' at Races."

"the world's . . . spectacular presentation": Letter from Henderson, 1935 Air Races folder, CHC, HSPD.

but close: In *HWF*, page 99, Thaden writes that by 1935, the Depression and other missteps had hit the Thadens with "a stiff wallop."

185 *"And he didn't . . . job for nothing"*: WFL, 235.

off the ground in Burbank: "L.A. Crash Kills Bendix Racer; Howard 1st at Cleveland," *Los Angeles Herald Express*, August 30, 1935.

186 *and she knew it*: "Air Race Score," *Los Angeles Examiner*, August 31, 1935.

187 *"Where's that man, Roscoe?"*: Details of Howard and Turner's race into Cleveland come from the *LAT, CPD, Cleveland News* and *Cleveland Press.*

Chapter 31: On the Sidelines

190 *in the nose:* The image of the new Beechcraft first appeared in the *WE* on June 29, 1932.

191 *in recent weeks:* Nichols estimated in *WFL* that they flew one thousand passengers that Sunday; the *NYT* put the number at eighteen hundred.

the plane burst into flames: News accounts of the crash and Nichols's personal account in her memoir differ on one detail: Nichols says Hublitz climbed through the hole in the cockpit, but at least one news story says he also was thrown from the plane.

192 *"Dear Rufus . . . sidelines for long":* Telegram from Earhart to Nichols, October 22, 1935, AE Papers, Marian Stabler Collection, IWASM.

Chapter 32: The Chance of a Lifetime

193 *for her that winter:* "A Woman's New York," *Louisville Courier-Journal,* December 15, 1935.

"Right now . . . to be a person": "Amelia Earhart Resting; Trying to 'Be Herself,'" *Dayton Daily News,* August 25, 1935.

194 *offered her two thousand dollars:* Elliott proposal to Earhart, May 18, 1935, President Elliott's Correspondence with GPP and AE, AE Papers, Purdue University.

"Even my . . . call me Miss Earhart": "Amelia Leaves Air to Guide Purdue Girls in Careers," *Lafayette Journal and Courier,* November 8, 1935.

questions of her own: AE, "Purdue University Questionnaire for Women Students, 1934–35," AOE Papers, SLRC.

put up forty thousand dollars: Letter from Elliott to Earhart, March 20, 1936, President Elliott's Correspondence with GPP and AE, AE Papers, Purdue University.

196 *two men on board:* Details of Dewey Noyes's crash come from "2 Flyers Killed at Nunda; Plane Rams Hill in Fog," *Rochester Democrat and Chronicle,* December 12, 1935; "18 Questioned in Air Deaths," *Rochester Democrat and Chronicle,* December 21, 1935; "Noyes, Pilot, Is Killed in Plane Crash," *CPD,* December 13, 1935; U.S. Department of Commerce press release, April 19, 1936, IWASM.

197 *"I think we . . . don't you?":* HWF, 109.

Chapter 33: We Are Going to Fly

198 *almost said no:* HWF, 109.

199 *beat Earhart:* Pat Thaden Webb interview, Bendix Collection, NASM.

"sensationally fast": "Bendix Race List Grows," *LAT*, August 20, 1936.

201 *"We are going . . . we will win it":* "Race Is Business Affair, Not Stunt, to Louise Thaden," *WE*, September 5, 1936.

Chapter 34: Splinters and a Grease Spot

202 *two hours and forty-five minutes:* "Howard and Wife Set Chicago-N.Y. Air Mark of 2 Hrs. 45 Minutes," *Chicago Tribune*, September 2, 1936.

no Roscoe Turner: Details about Roscoe Turner's ill-fated trip across the country for the Bendix race come from multiple sources, including the *LAT* and the *Gallup Independent*, August 31, 1936.

203 *Bad country:* "A Sinister Land Claimed the Wrecked Airliner," *NYT*, September 15, 1929.

204 *a different man:* "Col. Turner Crashes in New Mexico," *LAT*, August 31, 1936.

"I'm pretty shaky": "Turner Hurt in Plane, Out of Air Races," *Santa Rosa Press Democrat*, September 1, 1936.

"Splinters ... I'm not, too": "Turner Hurt, Returns Here," *LAT*, September 1, 1936.

Chapter 35: Goodbye, Darling

205 *"Bless Mother ... Mother"*: "Breaking Air Records No Novelty for This Woman Flyer," *St. Louis Post-Dispatch*, September 8, 1936.

gathered at ten thirty: HWF, 112.

private weather services: LT interview, 1971, PTW Family Files.

"generally good": "3 Air Teams Off on Race to Coast," *NYT*, September 4, 1936.

206 *got off first*: The *New York Post*, on September 4, 1936, published the exact time that each flier in the Bendix race took off.

hadn't checked: "Luck with Flier," WE, September 5, 1936.

"Goodbye, darling ... will you?": HWF, 112.

"Good luck": Jean Adams and Margaret Kimball, *Heroines of the Sky* (New York: Doubleday, Doran, 1942), 132.

207 *5:56 a.m.*: Accounts over the years have stated different takeoff times, but the local press in the next day's papers recorded it as 5:56 a.m.

stormy: Details about Jacobson's crash come from his first-person accounts given to three different newspapers: "Pilot Unaware Plane Exploded, Tells of Miraculous Leap," *Albuquerque Journal*, September 5, 1936; "Nerve Unshaken by Narrow Escape from Death, Flier Heads to Races," *WE*, September 5, 1934; and "Pilot Tells Close Call When Plane Blows Up," *LAT*, September 6, 1936.

Chapter 36: Sky Ghosts

209 *vibration in the plane's propeller*: Details about *Mister Mulligan*'s crash come from several sources, including Columbia University's oral history of Ben and Maxine Howard, April 1960; on-the-ground reporting and first-day news coverage of the crash in "Crownpoint Crash Victims Gain in Struggle to Survive," *Gallup Independent*, September 5, 1936; "Go-Grease Benny Howard," *Saturday Evening Post*, September 2, 1939; and Don Pratt, "Damned Good Airplanes: The Ben Howard Story," *Sport Flying* (August and October 1967), a two-part story about Benny Howard's career that included interviews with both Benny and Maxine.

210 *"No place to land"*: Ben Howard, oral history, 47, Columbia University, Special Collections.

211 *Sky ghosts:* "Crownpoint Crash Victims Gain in Struggle to Survive."

Chapter 37: A Woman Couldn't Win

212 *"Blanche . . . awake?":* This and other quotes from inside the plane come from *HWF*, 112 and 115.

213 *"What . . . a potato race?":* Ibid., 116.

214 *eleven-minute stop:* "Misses Death by Narrow Margin," *WE*, September 5, 1936.

215 *"I wonder . . . done wrong now":* HWF, 118.

"I'm afraid . . . won the Bendix": Thaden's and Blanche's recollection of this quote are slightly different, but Blanche never wavered in hers, repeating the same version of this quote over and over again for decades—in speeches, news stories, and oral histories—even while Henderson was still alive.

"So . . . couldn't win, eh?": HWF, 119.

"Congratulations . . . home town": Bendix victory telegrams, September 1936, LTC, NASM.

216 *"We won"*: Telegram from Thaden to her mother, Bendix victory
telegrams, September 1936, LTC, NASM.

Chapter 38: Disappointments, Dedication, and Courage

219 *"If a woman ... skirts or trousers"*: "Air Successes Open New Fields
to Women," *LAT*, September 8, 1936.

220 *"As ... more will enter"*: "Women's Timidity Undesirable Habit,
Amelia Earhart Asserts," *Binghamton Press and Sun-Bulletin*,
December 16, 1935.

221 *have to be perfect*: "Amelia Set for Flight to Howland Isle," *Oakland
Post-Enquirer*, March 19, 1937.

"You have . . . everything to lose": Thaden recounted this scene
in two different places, her memoir, *HWF*, 150, and an article
she wrote for the journal *Air Facts* in July 1970 titled "Amelia."
In each, the dialogue differs slightly, but the sentiment
is the same. These quotes come from the *Air Facts*
account.

"Women must ... challenge to others": Statement from Earhart,
1937 World Flight Attempt One, AE Papers, Purdue
University.

222 *wanted to stop her*: "Washington Bans Paris Air Race as Risking a Needless Loss of Life," *NYT*, May 18, 1937.

"About 200 miles out": The Earhart radio log was released at the time and published in the *NYHT*. It also appears in full in Record Group 237, National Archives.

223 *"That of a . . . close to breaking"*: Bellarts Papers, National Archives.

Three thousand people: "Navy Ends Search for Miss Earhart," *NYT*, July 19, 1939.

224 *"a greater ability . . . meet a challenge"*: "Women Best for Space, Pioneering Aviatrix Says," *Washington Post*, August 16, 1959.

"When spaceships . . . be flying them": WFL, 314.

225 *"Disappointments . . . defeat, after defeat"*: LT interview, 1971, PTW Family Files.

227 *"I have never . . . nor will I ever"*: Letter from Thaden to her daughter, June 6, 1956, PTW Family Files.

Index

A

air fields, 25, 28-29, 34, 37, 39, 43,
  47, 78, 85, 91, 202

Air-marking piloting, 185,
  195-96

airplanes
  American Girl, 27-28, 34-35, 40,
    42-45, 49
  Avian biplane, 88
  Beechcraft, 190, 199-201, 207,
    212, 214
  Curtiss Condors, 185
  Fairchild seaplane, 53
  Friendship, 65-68, 70, 72
  Gee Bee, 151-53, 155-59, 168-69,
    186-87
  Ken-Royce, 88
  Kinner Airster, 19

Lockheed *Akita*, 118-19, 124-27,
  136-37
Lockheed *Electra*, 194, 199
Lockheed *Vega*, 88
Rearwin, 88-89, 104
Sikorsky Flying Boat, *The
  Dawn*, 25, 38, 43, 45, 48
Spirit of St. Louis, 29
Swallow, 89
Thaden Metal Aircraft, 56-57,
  84
Travel Air, 8, 10-12, 84, 89, 91,
  98
air races
  Amelia Earhart trophy, 150
  Bendix Trophy race, 3, 133-34,
    154, 174-75, 184-88, 198-201,
    208-16, 219

air races (*cont.*)

    Dole Air Race, 39

    Ford Reliability Tour, 9-10

    National Air Races, 2, 75, 77, 85,
        184-85

    National Women's Air Derby,
        Powder Puff Derby, 90-91,
        93-97, 99-108

    New York–to–Los Angeles
        Derby, 80

    Orteig Prize, 25, 27, 31

    Phillips Trophy race, 155

    Thompson Trophy race, 130,
        151, 175

    women's national air meet,
        Dayton, 172

    women's race, Los Angeles to
        Cleveland, 85-87

B

Barnes, Florence "Pancho,"
    89

Beech, Walter and Olive, 9-12,
    54-55, 88-89, 101, 189-90,
    197-98, 205, 213

Bendix, Vincent, 130-35

C

Chamberlin, Clarence, 120, 123

Chapman, Sam, 18-20, 71

Coli, François, 26-28

crashes and failures, 1-2, 18, 26,
    39-40, 44-45, 48, 57-58, 80-81,
    98, 117-19, 126-27, 130, 135-38,
    157-60, 169-70, 173, 175-77,
    186-87, 191-92, 203-4, 209-11

Crosley, Powel, Jr., 118, 120-21

Crosson, Marvel, 89, 92, 97-100,
    106, 214

D

Dole, James, 39

Doolittle, Jimmy, 134, 153

E

Earhart, Amelia "A.E.," 17-22,
    61-72, 80-81, 85-86, 90-93,
    95-96, 100-102, 104-5, 110-11,
    114-16, 139-44, 166-67, 178-82,
    186-88, 193-96, 198-99, 202,
    206-7, 219-24

Elder, Ruth, 33-46, 49-52, 89-90,
    95, 99, 104, 225

F

Fairchild, Sherman, 53-54

Fonck, René, 25-26

G

Goldsborough, Brice "Goldy," 10, 46-47, 49

Gordon, Lou, 60, 63, 65-66, 69-70

Granville, Zantford Delbert, 151-53, 168-69

Grayson, Frances, "Flying Matron," 37-40, 42, 45-49, 214

H

Haldeman, George, 34, 36, 40, 42-45, 49

Halliburton, Erle, 99-100, 106

Hart, Beryl, 117

Henderson, Cliff, 75-86, 99-100, 105, 108, 128-32, 143-44, 150, 154-55, 159-60, 167-77, 179, 183-85, 215, 226

Hoover, Herbert, 40

Howard, Benny, 168, 174-75, 183, 187-88, 199-202, 205-11

K

Klingensmith, Florence, 147-50, 154-60

L

League for Fostering Genius, 50

Lindbergh, Charles, 28-31, 40, 60, 106, 130, 148

M

Marsalis, Frances, 161-62, 172-74, 214

McPhetridge, Louise. *See* Thaden, Louise

McQueen, Elizabeth Lippincott, 85-86, 109

N

Nichols, Ruth "Rufus," 13-16, 52-54, 62-63, 80, 88-90, 104-5, 110-11, 117-27, 135-38, 140, 143, 164-65, 179, 185, 191-92, 223-25

Ninety-Nines, women aviators, 110-11, 135, 163, 171-72, 178-79

Noyes, Blanche, 89, 92-93, 100, 196-99, 202, 206-7, 212-15

Nungesser, Charles, 26-29

O

Orteig, Raymond, 23-25, 27-28, 31

P

Penn School of Aviation, 111

Putnam, George Palmer, 59-60, 62-65, 72, 80-81, 114-18, 139-40, 142-43, 180-81, 193-94

R

Railey, Hilton Howell, 60-61, 63, 72, 121-24, 142-43

Rasche, Thea, 62

Rogers, Harry, 15-16, 53-54

S

Snook, Neta, 17-18

Stoner, Winifred Sackville, 50-51

Stultz, Wilmer "Bill," 46-47, 60, 63, 65, 67-68

T

Thaden, Herbert von, 56-58

Thaden, Louise, 7-8, 10, 55-58, 81-93, 95-97, 101-7, 110-13, 119, 128-29, 161-63, 172-73, 184-85, 195-202, 205-7, 212-16, 219-20, 225-28

transatlantic crossing, 23-31, 33-36, 40-42, 45-47, 49-50, 60, 64-70, 120-25, 139-44

transpacific crossing, 180-82

Turner, Jack, 8, 10-11, 87

Turner, Roscoe, 168, 174-76, 183, 185-88, 199-205

W

Warren, D. C., 55

women, treatment and attitudes
     towards, 3, 8, 54, 61-62,
     64, 79, 85, 91-92, 99, 109,
     111, 154, 163-64, 167-68,
     171-72, 174, 179, 183,
     219

Women's International Association of Aeronautics (WIAA),
     85

Wright, Orville, 56